CHERRY GOOD was born and raised in the settled districts of England and has been striving ever since to contradict her upbringing by exploring the wild places of the earth. She has been chased by aggressive ostriches on the Ningaloo Reef of Western Australia, had close encounters of the uncomfortable kind with rattlesnakes in the Mojave Desert, and had her supper eaten by black bears in the Californian High Sierra.

Like John Muir, Cherry Good is more interested in being out there experiencing it than in reading theoretical studies. She left an academic career and a cosy country cottage for the wide open spaces and hasn't regretted it for a moment. Her comprehensive knowledge of Muir's life and work and her heartfelt admiration for the man himself – his enthusiasm for the wild places of the earth – means she is amply qualified to follow his trail, by road and rail and air, but most of all on foot, walking in Muir's beloved Yosemite, in the Arizona desert, in Canada and in Scotland.

Her need for wilderness is equalled only by her fondness for chocolate labradors, freshly caught fish cooked over an open fire, her three daughters laughing together, and the scent of the high desert after rain – preferably all at the same time. When she tears herself away periodically from a close acquaintance with the world's mosquito population, she comes back to the Scottish Highlands or to her Devon roots, where she still manages to lose her way on Dartmoor.

John Muir wrote 'I care to live only to entice people to look at Nature's loveliness'. If *On the Trail of John Muir* has this effect, Cherry Good will be very happy.

On the Trail of John Muir

CHERRY GOOD

Luath Press Limited
EDINBURGH
www.luath.co.uk

First Edition 2000
Reprinted 2001
Reprinted 2006

ISBN (10): 0-946487-62-6
ISBN (13): 978-0-946487-62-2

The paper used in this book is neutral-sized and recyclable. It is made from
elemental chlorine-free pulps sourced from renewable forests.

Printed and bound by
Bell & Bain Ltd., Glasgow

Typeset in 10.5 point Sabon

Illustrations by Anthony Fury

This book is dedicated to Jo and Sarah and Rachel
for being themselves,
to Jon for being with me On the Trail
and to Freddo just for being

Acknowledgements

While *On the Trail of John Muir*, I made so many new friends and received so much help and encouragement that it's difficult to mention everyone – but here are most of the people I want to thank.

In California, a special thank you to Harold and Jan Wood for spending yet more time on John Muir, and for the best Thai food I've had. To the staff of the John Muir National Historic Site in Martinez – notably Phyllis Shaw and Dave Blackburn – and to the archivists at the Holt-Atherton Department of Special Collections, my warm appreciation for your time and patience, particularly to Janene Ford of Holt-Atherton for her mailing of photographs.

In Wisconsin, gratitude goes to Jamie Powell, who took time off during her busy day to talk about her famous ancestor and to walk me around the Madison sites connected with John Muir. A special acknowledgement to Erik and Maria Brynildson for conversation and hospitality beyond the bounds of friendship, to Maurice and Mary Kearns for their patience in allowing me to crawl all over their farm taking photographs, to Millie Stanley for sharing with me her view of John Muir's 'world', and to Faith Miracle of the Wisconsin Academy of Sciences, Arts and Letters. I would also like to single out Nina and Charles Bradley of The Aldo Leopold Foundation in Baraboo, whose reminiscences, kindness and hospitality will never be forgotten, and who also permitted me to reproduce one of my favourite photographs of John Muir.

In Canada, the home provided by Doris Scholl, and the advice and assistance from Ron Knight, made the Meaford section of my *Trail* a particularly memorable and rewarding one. Also invariably helpful and welcoming were the Canadian Friends of John Muir, notably Scott Cameron, Jack Morgan, Bruce Cox, Robert and Lorraine Burcher, and Stephan Fuller. Dr Jim Butler of the University of Alberta was a mine of information, and my thanks go also to Connie Bresnahan of Alberta, to Ann McGrath, to Doug Grant, Mayor of Meaford, and to the St Vincent Township Council.

In Scotland, I acknowledge the useful information provided by the John Muir Trust and Dunbar's John Muir Association, and in particular the advice and friendship of Graham White and the long-distance good nature of my publisher, Gavin MacDougall, during much transatlantic communication while I was *On the Trail* in the United States.

Contents

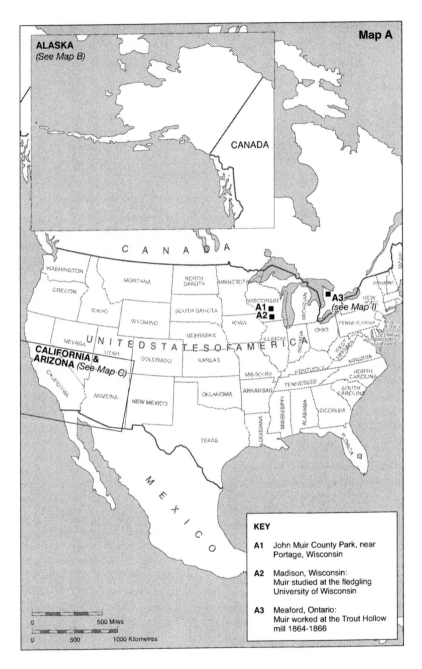

Map A

ALASKA
(See Map B)

CANADA

CANADA

WASHINGTON
OREGON
MONTANA
IDAHO
WYOMING
NORTH DAKOTA
SOUTH DAKOTA
MINNESOTA
IOWA
NEBRASKA
WISCONSIN
MICHIGAN
NEW YORK
MAINE
VERMONT

A1 ■
A2 ■
A3 ■
(see Map I)

**CALIFORNIA &
ARIZONA** *(See Map C)*

NEVADA
UTAH
CALIFORNIA
ARIZONA
COLORADO
KANSAS
NEW MEXICO
OKLAHOMA
TEXAS

U N I T E D   S T A T E S   O F   A M E R I C A

ILLINOIS
INDIANA
OHIO
PENNSYLVANIA
WEST VIRGINIA
VIRGINIA
KENTUCKY
MISSOURI
TENNESSEE
NORTH CAROLINA
SOUTH CAROLINA
ARKANSAS
MISSISSIPPI
ALABAMA
GEORGIA
LOUISIANA
FLORIDA

M E X I C O

KEY

A1   John Muir County Park, near
         Portage, Wisconsin

A2   Madison, Wisconsin:
         Muir studied at the fledgling
         University of Wisconsin

A3   Meaford, Ontario:
         Muir worked at the Trout Hollow
         mill 1864-1866

0   500 Miles

0   500   1000 Kilometres

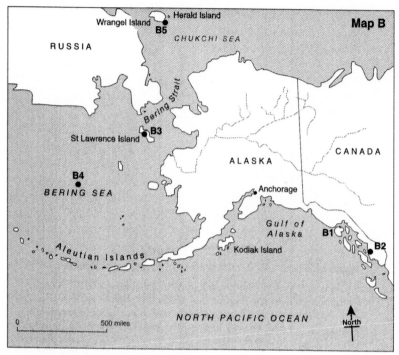

Alaska and Glacier Bay National Park

KEY

B1 Glacier Bay National Park and Muir Glacier

B2 Wrangell, the starting point for many of Muir's Alaskan explorations

B3 Lawrence Island, visited by the Harriman Expedition in 1899

B4 Bering Sea, where John Burroughs suffered so badly from seasickness

B5 Wrangel Island/Herald Island, visited by the Thomas Corwin Expedition in 1881, searching for the lost ship Jeannette

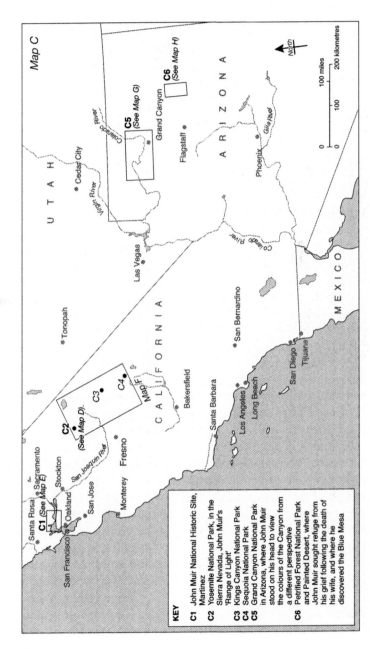

Map C

KEY

C1 John Muir National Historic Site, Martinez
C2 Yosemite National Park, in the Sierra Nevada, John Muir's 'Range of Light'
C3 Kings Canyon National Park
C4 Sequoia National Park
C5 Grand Canyon National Park in Arizona, where John Muir stood on his head to view the colours of the Canyon from a different perspective
C6 Petrified Forest National Park and Painted Desert, where John Muir sought refuge from his grief following the death of his wife, and where he discovered the Blue Mesa

California and Arizona

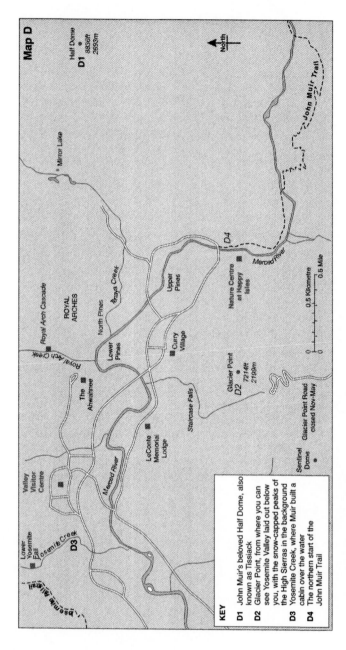

Map D

Half Dome
D1 *
8836ft
2693m

North

John Muir Trail

Mirror Lake

D4

Merced River

Royal Arch Cascade

ROYAL
ARCHES

Tenaya Creek

North Pines

Upper
Pines

Nature Centre
at Happy Isles

0   0.5 Kilometre
0   0.5 Mile

Royal Arch Creek

The
Ahwahnee

Lower
Pines

Curry
Village

Glacier Point
D2 *
7214ft
2199m

Staircase Falls

Glacier Point Road
closed Nov–May

Merced River

LeConte
Memorial
Lodge

Valley
Visitor
Centre

Sentinel
Dome

Lower
Yosemite
Fall

Yosemite Creek

D3

Pohono Trail

KEY

D1 John Muir's beloved Half Dome, also
    known as Tissiack
D2 Glacier Point, from where you can
    see Yosemite Valley laid out below
    you, with the snow-capped peaks of
    the High Sierras in the background
D3 Yosemite Creek, where Muir built a
    cabin over the water
D4 The northern start of the
    John Muir Trail

Yosemite Valley, showing Glacier Point and the northern start of the John Muir Trail

Map E

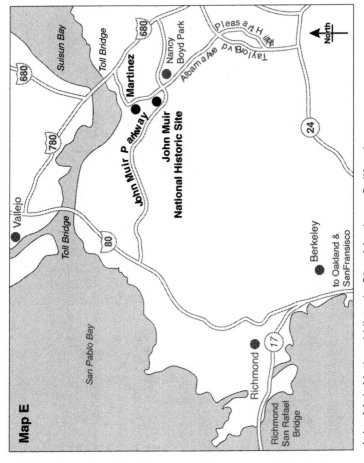

John Muir National Historic Site, Martinez, California

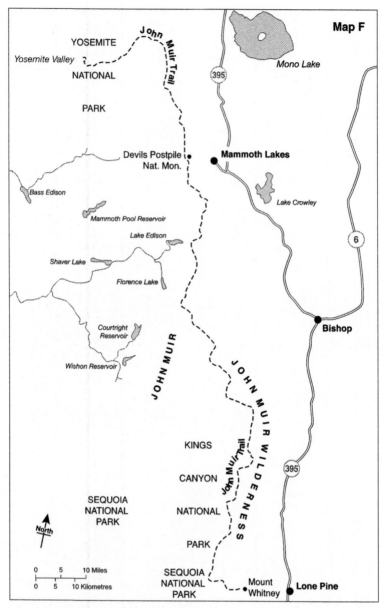

The John Muir Trail, California

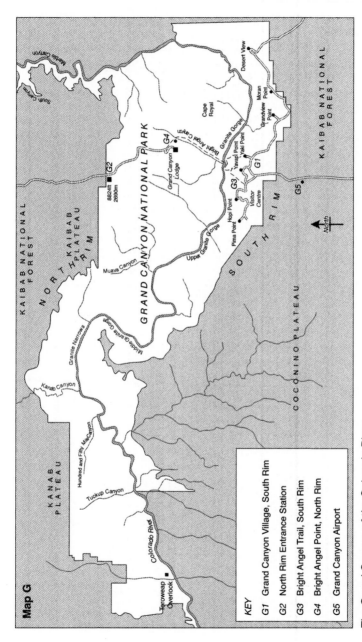

Map G

KEY

G1 Grand Canyon Village, South Rim
G2 North Rim Entrance Station
G3 Bright Angel Trail, South Rim
G4 Bright Angel Point, North Rim
G5 Grand Canyon Airport

The Grand Canyon of the Colorado River

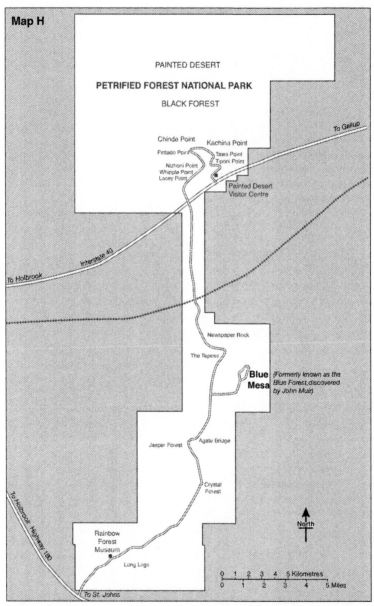

Map H

PAINTED DESERT

PETRIFIED FOREST NATIONAL PARK

BLACK FOREST

To Gallup

Chinde Point   Kachina Point

Pintado Point   Tawa Point
                 Tiponi Point

Nizhoni Point
Whipple Point
Lacey Point

Painted Desert
Visitor Centre

Interstate 40

To Holbrook

Newspaper Rock

The Tepees

Blue Mesa *(Formerly known as the Blue Forest, discovered by John Muir)*

Jasper Forest   Agate Bridge

Crystal Forest

North

To Holbrook Highway 180

Rainbow Forest Museum

Long Logs

To St Johns

| 0 | 1 | 2 | 3 | 4 | 5 Kilometres |
| 0 | 1 | 2 | 3 | 4 | 5 Miles |

Petrified Forest National Park and the Painted Desert, Arizona.

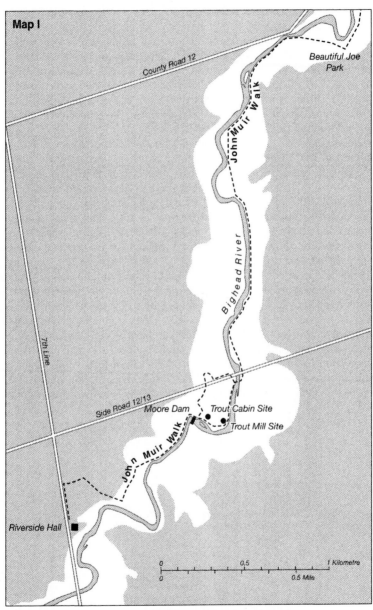

Map I

County Road 12

Beautiful Joe Park

John Muir Walk

Bighead River

7th Line

Side Road 12/13

Moore Dam   Trout Cabin Site

Trout Mill Site

John Muir Walk

Riverside Hall

0   0.5   1 Kilometre

0   0.5 Mile

The John Muir Walk through Trout Hollow, Meaford, Ontario

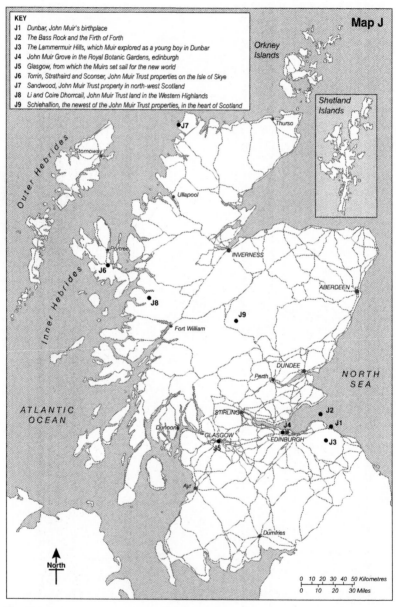

KEY
J1 Dunbar, John Muir's birthplace
J2 The Bass Rock and the Firth of Forth
J3 The Lammermuir Hills, which Muir explored as a young boy in Dunbar
J4 John Muir Grove in the Royal Botanic Gardens, edinburgh
J5 Glasgow, from which the Muirs set sail for the new world
J6 Torrin, Strathaird and Sconser, John Muir Trust properties on the Isle of Skye
J7 Sandwood, John Muir Trust property in north-west Scotland
J8 Li and Coire Dhorrcail, John Muir Trust land in the Western Highlands
J9 Schiehallion, the newest of the John Muir Trust properties, in the heart of Scotland

Map J

Orkney Islands

Shetland Islands

Outer Hebrides
Stornoway
Thurso
Ullapool
Inner Hebrides
Portree
J6
J7
INVERNESS
ABERDEEN
J8
Fort William
J9
DUNDEE
Perth
NORTH SEA
ATLANTIC OCEAN
STIRLING
J2
Dunoon
J4
J1
GLASGOW
EDINBURGH
J5
J3
Ayr
Dumfries

North

0 10 20 30 40 50 Kilometres
0 10 20 30 Miles

Scotland

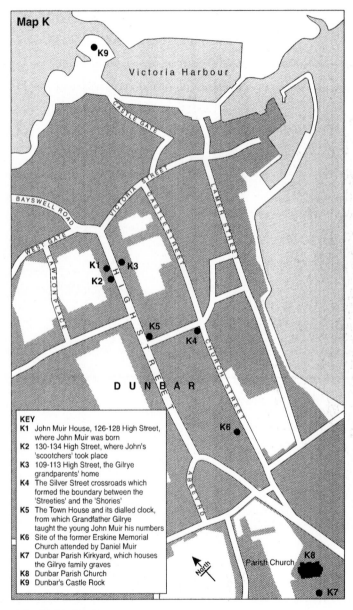

Map K

Victoria Harbour

K9

CASTLE GATE

BAYSWELL ROAD

VICTORIA STREET

CASTLE STREET

LAMER STREET

WEST GATE

LAWSON PLACE

K1 K3
K2

HIGH STREET

K5
K4

CHURCH STREET

D U N B A R

K6

ABBEY RD

North

Parish Church

K8

K7

KEY
K1 John Muir House, 126-128 High Street, where John Muir was born
K2 130-134 High Street, where John's 'scootchers' took place
K3 109-113 High Street, the Gilrye grandparents' home
K4 The Silver Street crossroads which formed the boundary between the 'Streeties' and the 'Shories'
K5 The Town House and its dialled clock, from which Grandfather Gilrye taught the young John Muir his numbers
K6 Site of the former Erskine Memorial Church attended by Daniel Muir
K7 Dunbar Parish Kirkyard, which houses the Gilrye family graves
K8 Dunbar Parish Church
K9 Dunbar's Castle Rock

John Muir's Dunbar

John Muir family on porch at Martinez

Foreword

I WROTE THIS BOOK ON THE ROAD, as I followed John Muir's trail from Scotland to the American Midwest, through the inland waters and forests of Canada and the lush humidity of America's Deep South to the glacial meadows and crystal lakes of California's High Sierra.

It wasn't easy. In my attempt to get as close as I could to the places which John Muir loved, I stayed in no hotels, slept in no comfortable beds. Each night, whether it rained or snowed or blew sand, I camped and wrote. In the Californian and Arizona deserts I slept on the bare earth without a tent, worried about rattlesnakes, and came into close contact with a tarantula. On my first visit to the High Sierra I fretted constantly about black bears. In the New Zealand autumn I relinquished any hope of ever being dry again, and in Australia I forded rising creeks and was chased by agressive ostriches – don't laugh, those powerful feet pack a helluva wallop, enough to break your leg and associated body parts.

But the bane of my life was – and still is – the mosquito. This insignificant-looking little monster with its harpoon inhabits many of the areas through which I travelled: Yosemite in springtime, the sand country of Wisconsin, the bogs and lakes and woods of Ontario, the southern states of the US. I yell and clutch and swat, then swell and scratch, becoming irrational with mosquito-hate. My admiration for John Muir and his apparent unconcern about mosquito bites reaches unprecedented heights, as I debate the rival merits of sleeping under the stars with the harpooneers versus locking myself into the truck.

When it comes down to the essentials, none of these inconveniences really matter. Even with the mosquitoes it's worth it, the

Even to the least-loved mosquitoes I gave many a meal, and told them to go in peace.

Journal entry,
Alaska, August 1880

*Sit down
in climbing,
and hear the
pines sing.*

Undated journal entry

privilege of being out there, seeing the desert bloom in springtime, Yosemite Falls shooting its snow-thawed torrents in rocketing cascades to the valley floor below, the yip-yip-yip of the coyote at dusk, the heat and buzz of high summer, the pristine stillness of deep winter in the mountains.

John Muir knew that each of us in our own way needs the wilderness, even when it frightens or discomforts us, and that each of us needs to find it for ourselves. *On the Trail of John Muir* provides an opportunity to do just that, following in the footsteps of a Scottish boy with no influence and little schooling who loved wild things and became determined to protect them. Use the book as your passport to his world – just watch out for those mosquitoes.

Introduction

IF YOU ASK A SCOT a question about John Muir, unless he's in the habit of climbing mountains or hails from Dunbar, he'll probably say 'John who?' If you ask the average American – if there is such a thing – he'll search the memory banks and possibly come up with some hazy school-days recollection of a connection with National Parks or the Sierra Club.

A Californian, however, particularly if the speaker is a walker, is prone to use the opportunity to launch into a lengthy discussion of the edited highlights of John Muir's life and achievements. In the case of Muir, this talkativeness can't be entirely attributed to the fabled willingness of Californians – and other Americans – to engage their fellow-beings in conversation. (You're familiar with the syndrome – sit down next to one and in five minutes flat you know their annual income, personal motivation and sexual preferences.) Many Californians *know* about Muir, his writing, mountain climbing and conservation work; they're proud of him, and they think of him as a fellow Californian.

But he wasn't. He was born in Scotland, in Dunbar, in 1838. Yet, outside Dunbar, he's relatively unknown in his native land, and people in the rest of Britain generally remain unaware of his existence. How has this come about?

First of all, he didn't stay in Scotland long enough to be easily identified as a Scot. His family emigrated to the United States in 1849, when he was a boy of eleven, and he didn't revisit his childhood home until he was in his fifties. By that time he was a well-known figure in the US, fêted wherever he went and claimed by many Americans as one of their own. Yet he never thought of himself as anything but a Scot, retaining his Scottish accent and ironic sense of humour and pursuing a life-long love

Living artificially, we seldom see much of our real selves.

Explorations in the Great Tuolumne Canyon, first published in the *Overland Monthly*, August 1873 affair with the poetry of Robert Burns – 'wherever a Scotsman goes, there goes Burns'. His early formative years were spent on the shores of the Firth of Forth and exploring the Lammermuir Hills, and it didn't take much to bring back those memories of Scotland, however far away he was. Nearing the Florida coast, he catches a breath of salt air and is at once back in Dunbar, 'its rocky coast, winds and waves'; dozing on a long transcontinental rail journey, he hears a Scottish accent and leaps to his feet to welcome a fellow countryman, spending the rest of the night in animated conversation.

Secondly, he achieved fame in a distant country, separated from Scotland by the broad Atlantic and also by differing attitudes towards the preservation of wild places. When, in the 1870s, Muir began his fight to protect the forests and mountains of California from commercial inroads, the idea of conservation was a novelty to the American public. In Scotland, where sheep grazing still ruled the glens, it was virtually unheard of. California was too far away, and wilderness conservation for its own sake was too alien a concept to be taken seriously in Britain. No wonder that few people knew the name of John Muir.

It is only during recent decades that conservation has achieved high profile status throughout the world and that John Muir has begun to achieve some recognition in the country of his birth – much of it in Dunbar. In 1976 Dunbar created the John Muir Country Park, followed by John Muir House (Muir's birthplace) in 1981, and in 1983 the John Muir Trust was formed, to promote the Muir conservation ethic and conserve the wild areas of Scotland.

So who was this man John Muir, how did he achieve fame in America, and why should Scotland be proud to claim him as her son? Spending his teenage years in Wisconsin, tramping through nineteenth century America, exploring the mountains and forests of the west, he became convinced that government protection was essential to preserve the country's wild places from the inroads of lumbering, farming, railroad building, and a hundred other commercial interests. Writing, lobbying, talking to anyone who would listen, he gradually persuaded enough people to share his views, and those people in turn persuaded the American government to do something, to pass protective legislation. Prodded by Muir and his supporters, Teddy Roosevelt created one hundred and forty million acres of National Forest, five National Parks and twenty three National Monuments. In 1892 Muir and friends formed the Sierra Club, which continues today to mobilise support for wilderness conservation.

In particular, Muir achieved support and fame by publishing a large number of articles in support of conservation, and kept copious notes and journals – some published as books during his lifetime, but mostly issued after his death – all of which have kept his theories and arguments alive and accessible today (see the bibliography for details).

Wilderness conservation was not his only claim to fame. In his youth, he was a gifted inventor and undoubtedly could have achieved fame and fortune in the commercial world, had he chosen to. He was a dedicated botanist and naturalist and was several times offered academic positions, but he preferred the natural world to the classroom. Studying the effects of glacial activity in the Californian mountains, he put forward glaciation theories which confounded the orthodox thinking of his day – theories which subsequently proved correct. Fruit farming in the Alhambra Valley of Northern California, he made such a success of the ranch that he never again needed to worry about his bank balance. And he climbed; his favourite self-description was 'mountaineer' and he never tired of the exhilaration that comes with increasing altitude. He made solo ascents of Mount Ritter, Mount Whitney and many others, frequently without the help of ropes or any other aids, and certainly without any of the lightweight gear that modern climbers take for granted. He walked and climbed wearing everyday work clothes, without a coat and often without blankets, preferring to travel light, and with nails cobbled into the soles of his shoes in icy weather.

All of this is, to say the least, somewhat daunting if you're trying to follow in the footsteps of John Muir. In the western states of the US, he has achieved hero status. There are statues of Muir, numerous places named after him, a John Muir National Historic

Site in Martinez an annual John Muir Day in California in 1964 and 1998 the US Post Office issued commemorative Muir stamps. How can anyone hope to achieve what he achieved, climb all those mountains, save all those forests and valleys, encompass as many interests as he did? It's too easy to 'dismiss' him as exceptional, to raise him up on a pedestal and convince ourselves that there's no way in which we could achieve anything like he did.

That's the way I felt when I started the research for this book. I had for a long time admired John Muir and his work, read everything he wrote, walked with the Sierra Club, explored the wilderness areas that he so loved and fought to protect. But I accorded him hero status, placed him up there on his pedestal, separate from the rest of us mere mortals. It wasn't until I started to read his unpublished journals, letters to his close friends, his wife and two daughters, that he became *real*, one of us, a man who was often lonely and scared, shivering and wet and hungry, doing the Highland Fling on a mountain top to keep hypothermia at bay, wrapping handkerchiefs around a little dog's paws on the Alaskan glacier to protect them from the lacerating affects of the ice. His friends and family, particularly his sisters, complained that he always talked too much; listening to anyone practising the piano drove him crazy; he was allergic to poison oak and city pavements; he was *human*.

> *Only by going in silence, without baggage, can one truly get into the heart of the wilderness. All other travel is mere dust and hotels and baggage and chatter.*
>
> Letter from John Muir to his wife Louie, July 1888

As long as I left him on the pedestal, thought of him as exceptional, even superhuman, I could delude myself that my attempts to preserve wild places were futile, that I could have little or no affect. Eventually (I'm a slow learner) I realised, of course, that John Muir felt the same way but didn't let that stop him. Throughout his conservation attempts, from the early 'tramping' days in Yosemite to the public Muir of the Hetch Hetchy campaign, there was often little or no prospect of success, yet Muir, one individual, plodded on – and made a difference. Lawrence Downing, past President of the Sierra Club, commented that Muir 'taught us much about citizen activism and its power to move governments'.

On the Trail of John Muir is my attempt to portray a man whose world view ought to be known beyond the bounds of California and Dunbar, and also to say: if you haven't done so already, get out there and take a look at it. Walk or climb or camp in the great outdoors, not to 'peak bag' or see how fast you can do it – just to look at it and let it work on you; then, and only then will you fully appreciate what John Muir was talking about. Watching wilderness programmes on TV won't do it and nor will reading about it, however stunning the photographs.

While shepherding in the Sierra, Muir came face-to-face with a bear. Writing of the encounter in *My First Summer in the Sierra*, he presented it in a humorous way, although at the time he probably found it alarming rather than amusing. It can feel scary out there – many of us are unaccustomed to being out of earshot of neighbours – but you're unlikely to come to any harm, particularly from black bears who are far more interested in your supper than in you. On my first winter visit to Yosemite, some years ago, the rangers quizzed me on my knowledge of black bear behaviour before I pitched my tent. 'If they come up to you while you're eating,' they told me, 'don't let them take the food off your plates. Bang two metal dishes together or shout at them, tell them off in a loud voice. They don't like that. I say, 'Bad bear, stop that!' That usually stops them.'

At the time, I wrote in my diary

I don't much care for that 'usually'. What happens when things aren't usual? I practise saying 'bad bear' in an authoritative voice but am afraid I won't do so well when confronted by an actual bad bear, so take two tin plates to bed with me, just to be on the safe side. My tiny tent is pitched in a small patch of cleared ground, snow all around, and as the temperature falls well below freezing I wriggle into all my clothes, including down jacket, and then into the sleeping bag, the snow continuing to patter down on the tent throughout darkness and staying well into the next morning until the sun begins to make itself felt. I love waking during the night to hear the snow hitting the tent while I'm warm and snug in my layers and bag, and wonder how Muir managed without all these insulated goodies. Not so good leaving the tent to have a pee, though, taking my tin plates with me in case of bad bears. I must have looked a pretty sight – bright yellow too-large down jacket, brilliant turquoise ear-flapped hat, clashing green trousers and hefty boots, tin plates ready for clashing, crouching in the snowbound moonlight, head swivelling rapidly from right to left to search out advancing bad bears before they noticed me.

When you're out there, see the funny side of doing without home comforts, and take your time, just as Muir did:

I drifted about from rock to rock, from stream to stream. Where night found me, there I camped. When I discovered a new plant, I sat down beside it, for a minute or a day, to make its acquaintance and try to hear what it had to say.

In *Sacred Summits*: *John Muir's Greatest Climbs*, Graham White suggests that Muir's approach to nature was related to the quality of his experience, not the quantity. He was not interested in how many times he had climbed a specific peak or visited a particular lake, but in how it *felt*.

Muir transmitted this enthusiasm, this involvement, to many people he met. S. Hall Young, his missionary companion on many Alaskan trips, saw him as an inspiration – 'I sat at his feet' – and others felt the same. Robert Moran, engineer on the Alaskan river steamer Cassiar, was befriended by Muir; many years later, Moran presented to the state 10,000 acres of forest on Orcas Island in Puget Sound, crediting his conversations with Muir as his inspiration for the gift.

Muir seems to me very much the down-to-earth realist. His prose may sometimes appear somewhat dated, his language too 'flowery' for contemporary taste; his character was anything but. He's a pragmatist – if one avenue appears blocked, he searches immediately for another, never losing sight of his goals. And when he loses a fight, as with Hetch Hetchy, he puts it behind him and turns to the next battle.

Many people and belief systems would like to claim John Muir as essentially theirs. The Scots are proud to call him their son, Wisconsin sees him as spending his formative teenage years in the sand country of Fountain Lake and Hickory Hill, while the Canadian town of Meaford, where he spent a year and a half in the 1860s, argues that the Canadian sojourn was Muir's first extended wilderness experience, and therefore a turning point in his attitude towards the natural world. Alaska too has a claim, and Californians have taken Muir to their hearts, heaping honours on him, giving him an annual day of his own.

Christianity says he is theirs – after all, he was forever mentioning God's great works in nature – and there have been a number of claimings by other beliefs, Zen Budhism amongst them. Was he a Pantheist, someone who believes that the higher power lies in nature, not in church-bound religion? And is he best defined as a naturalist or a glaciologist, an inventor or a farmer, mountaineer or conservationist? What about brother, husband, father?

Each of these has put in a bid for John Muir, and perhaps each of them has a valid argument. But when it comes to the crux, does it matter? Why does he need to be defined, claimed, pigeon-holed? Can't he just be accepted as he was, the sum of all these parts and larger than any of them?

In writing this book, I used mainly Muir's own accounts – journals, essays, letters, and the autobiographical books covering his early years – many of them completed and published in maturity. Of his childhood and early wanderings, there is no other version. When it first came out, *The Story of My Boyhood and Youth* shocked many readers, with its portrayal of childhood deprivation and constant beatings, and some commentators queried whether the violence and suffering had been over stated. A comment in a letter to Muir from his sister Joanna confirmed otherwise: 'The portion relating to yourself and the family was read in tears, and I wished with all my heart it had not been so true.'

I have given a considerable percentage of the book to those youthful years in Scotland and in Wisconsin, because I believe those were his formative days. In Dunbar and at Fountain Lake Farm he learned to endure and to love the land, its creatures and its plants, for their own beauty, for themselves, not for the benefits that they yield to man.

The Canadian sojourn has generally been skimmed over by

biographers, since we have no journals for this period. Here, I have concentrated on the current situation in Meaford, Ontario, because of the recent publication of five 'new' Muir letters, the ensuing detective work on the Trout Hollow site, and the way in which the choices confronting Meaford residents now are also representative of the conservation debates of Muir's time. Those same debates which you can see in Meaford on a small scale are also raging in California's Yosemite Valley, where a proposal to restrict car access to the Valley in favour of shuttle buses is under scrutiny. In spring and summer, the Valley which Muir fought so hard to protect is now beseiged by heavy traffic, campgrounds, stores, and thousands of tourists every sunny day.

For the Yosemite years, we again have Muir's accounts, plus the reminiscences and letters of those who knew him, and the Alaskan trips and world tours are well documented, along with the 'public' Muir of the Roosevelt and Hetch Hetchy era. Less well documented are the years that Muir spent on the Martinez ranch, and there is a notable lack of information about his wife Louie, who was a very private person, fiercely protective of her daughters and supportive of her talkative and famous husband.

To everyone who is appalled at the use of the word 'Scotch' in some of the Muir quotations (and yes, of course I know it should be used only to describe the amber nectar), I can only apologise on Muir's behalf and say that, at the time when he was writing, the term was freely used to denote all things Scottish. In other words, I've quoted him verbatim rather than mess about with his language.

To avoid cluttering up the pages or distracting the eye with little numbers every few lines, there are no footnotes or endnotes. They'd only distract you from the main story, and if you want to read further, there's the bibliography. Unless I've indicated otherwise, the quotes are all Muir's, and the main frustration in compiling this book has been where to stop. The man had so many interests, so many facets to his personality, public and private, that to do him justice I should have written a thousand pages or more. So please forgive me if you're a Muir enthusiast and I've omitted your favourite anecdote or glossed over some happening which you feel is of particular importance. It doubtless is – they all are – but I had to stop somewhere. What I *have* tried to do is present John Muir as a fully-rounded person, not as a hero or a mountaineer or a father – although he was all of those and many more things too – but simply as a man. I hope you like him as much as I do.

Cherry Good
January 2000

CHAPTER I

Home in Scotland

NAKED EXCEPT FOR HIS billowing nightgown, a young boy stood on the edge of his dormer window, two storeys above the ground. Lowering himself carefully onto the sill, he hung first by one hand and then by one finger. Not content with this, he edged slowly up the steep slope of the roof, finding cracks to hold his fingers, until he could sit astride the peak, the freshening wind tugging at his nightgown and threatening to throw him off at any moment. At last he turned. Sliding carefully back down the slates to the safety of his attic room, he stood panting by the bed, his eyes shining with the excitement of this latest dare.

The boy was John Muir, who in manhood would become a renowned naturalist and conservationist of the world's wild places, but who always preferred to describe himself as a mountaineer. His early exploits on the roof of his parents' house in the Scottish town of Dunbar, his scrambles in the Lammermuir Hills above his home and on the crumbling sandstone ruins of Dunbar Castle, stood him in good stead when it came to climbing the high peaks of California's Sierra Nevada or the glaciers of Alaska.

Not that he believed he could repeat that rooftop dare, or 'scootcher', in later life. When at the age of fifty five he made a trip home to Dunbar, he took another look at the window and the angle of the roof and confessed that he didn't know how he'd done it as a boy and certainly couldn't do it again. This disbelief must have been shared by his younger brother David, who on that memorable summer night of their childhood scootcher tried to follow his brother's example and froze high on the roof, crying 'I canna get doon. Oh, I canna get

Wherever a Scotsman goes, there goes Burns.

Thoughts written on the birthday of Robert Burns, January 1906 doon.' Worried that their father might hear the cries and that retribution would surely follow, John called encouragingly to his brother, 'Dinna greet, Davie, dinna greet, I'll help ye doon. If you greet, fayther will hear, and gee us baith an awfu' skelping.' Balancing on the sill, he managed to drag David back into the attic bedroom above Dunbar's High Street.

You can still see the house where John and David Muir's scootcher took place, at 130-134 High Street. Like many buildings in the town, it has been substantially altered over the years, with an additional storey added in place of the dormer windows, and when in 1893 Muir returned to his boyhood home, he found it had been converted into the Lorne Hotel. It's still one of the largest buildings in the street, behind which the Muir children played in the ample rear garden, with its elm trees and birds' nests, the flower beds tended so lovingly by their mother, Anne, and a special bed of lilies belonging to John's aunt.

It was in this garden that the small boy first developed his love of plants and birdlife. In *The Story of My Boyhood and Youth*, he tells the sad tale of a pair of robins raising their young in one of the elm trees. Several soldiers from a visiting troop of the Scots Greys kept their horses in the Muir stables. One of them spied the nest, climbed the tree and rode away with the fledgling robins tucked inside his jacket, 'caring only for the few pennies the young songbirds would bring and the beer they would buy'. John and his brothers and sisters, listening to the screams of the bereaved robin parents, watching their anguished, futile attempts to save the babies, could not contain their grief and sobbed themselves to sleep that night.

John Muir House

John was born not in this large house but in the smaller one next door, 128 High Street, now called John Muir House, which has been restored to represent the house at the time of his birth in April 1838. The top flat, accessed by an external stairwell down the side alley, houses a small museum, with pictorial and audio-visual pre-sentations, and is open to the public daily between June and September (Tel. 01368 862585) and at other times by arrangement with Dunbar town guide Jim Thompson, 01368 864329. A typical eighteenth century small Dunbar house, in the Muirs' time it had cellars, coal-holes, a midden and outside privies, with all water collected from the town well-heads on the High Street. John's father, Daniel Muir, ran his business from the house, trading in grain, flour and meal, and the business flourished, enabling him in 1842 to buy the larger premises next door at what is now 130-134 High Street.

Daniel Muir was not born into prosperity. Shortly after his birth in Manchester in 1804, both his parents died, and he and his eleven year old sister Mary returned to their native Lanarkshire to live with relatives and to be treated, as far as we can ascertain, as farm servants. Here the young Daniel tried to find some respite from the monotony of his farm drudgery by carving small shapes from scraps of wood – a skill inherited by his son John – and by making himself a fiddle and singing the old Scots ballads that he loved. In the early years in Dunbar, John remembered his father singing and playing to the children: 'My first conscious memory is the singing of ballads, and I doubt not they will be ringing in my ears when I am dying.'

But soon the fiddle was put away and the singing stopped, for Daniel Muir had seen the light. At some stage during his Lanarkshire sojourn – Linnie Marsh Wolfe's Pulitzer Prize-win-ning biography of John Muir suggests it was at the age of fourteen – Daniel experienced a revelatory conversion to evangelical Presbyterianism and spent the rest of his life fighting for the souls of his fellow men and waging war against the devil. He came to believe that the briefest relaxation of watchfulness, the merest moment of inattention, could allow sin to enter in, and in partic-ular he considered it his bounden duty to prevent such sin from entering into his own children, those for whom he felt supremely responsible. To this end he whipped them for the slightest trans-gression, seeing it as a kindness to save them from the flames of hell, banned all forms of decoration, pictures, and even his wife's embroidery from the Dunbar house, and saw to it that all meals were taken in total silence, as befitted a sacrament.

A number of John Muir's biographers have seen his father as a cruel and insensitive man, imposing his fanatical zeal and iron will on helpless children, and so it certainly seems to us today, when Daniel Muir would have stood accused of child abuse and had his family removed from him. Even in his own time, his neighbours whispered about him as 'strange' and his father-in-law, David Gilrye, was greatly concerned when daughter Anne insisted on marrying a man of such fanatical religious beliefs. But we also need to remember that Daniel Muir, sadly misguided though he is to us, was a product of early bereavement and grinding poverty, and that he saw in evangelical religion his opportunity to make a difference in a world which otherwise gave him no influence whatsoever – an opportunity to share with others his revelatory vision and to set them on the path towards what he saw as their reward in the Hereafter. In doing so he beat his children, worked them so hard that their health often suffered, and forbade them many of the simple pleasures of childhood and youth.

When Daniel Muir was twenty one he left the hills for Glasgow, hoping to earn enough there to buy himself a passage to North America, but found many others like himself wandering the streets, a great mass of men chasing the few jobs available. In desperation, cold and hungry, he enlisted in one of the Scottish regiments, and in 1829 he was sent as a recruiting sergeant to the town of Dunbar. There he met and married a young heiress, who purchased his early release from the army, and whose rather shaky grain business he transformed into one of Dunbar's most successful stores by establishing a reputation for absolute fairness in his business dealings. But his new wife and child both died early in the marriage, and by 1833 he remarried, this time to Anne Gilrye, the daughter of David Gilrye, who opposed the marriage of his much-loved child to a man of such fanatical zeal.

In her new home at 128 High Street, on the premises of the grain and feed store, Anne learned that her husband considered all meals as sacraments, to be eaten in silence, that any form of adornment or decoration was forbidden under Daniel's interpretation of Christian scripture, and that she was expected to be solemn and silent for much of the time. Determined to be the dutiful wife, she gradually learned to accept these strictures, keeping her moments of gaiety and romanticism (she liked, for instance, to write and read poetry) for her parents and friends, and developing an inner strength, a centredness, an ability to endure in trying circumstances, which she transmitted to her son John and which he recognised as one of his most valuable characteristics.

Soon the children started to arrive. First Margaret in 1834, followed by Sarah's birth in 1836 and then John on 21 April 1838. After John came David in 1840, Daniel junior in 1843, the twins Mary and Annie in 1846, and the final daughter, Joanna, born in 1850 after the move to Wisconsin. Eight children, all of whom survived infancy and lived well into adulthood, an amazing achievement at that time, when high child mortality was an unpalatable fact of life. Anne Gilrye's parents, David and Margaret, had produced ten children, of whom only two, Margaret and Anne, survived to full adulthood. The remaining eight lay in the kirkyard, victims of 'white plague' – possibly diphtheria. No wonder that Anne's father was protective of her, doubting Daniel Muir's ability to make her a good husband, and feeling deeply the pain of parting when she left Dunbar for ever to join her husband in America.

David Gilrye bought a family plot in the Dunbar parish kirkyard and you can find the Gilrye family graves there. Go around to the right hand (west) side of the church, next to the tower, and turn down the gravel path which runs south-east and parallel to the wall. On your left you will see a large stone with an urn and then a little further on a large obelisk. Stand between these two markers and the Gilrye pair of headstones can be seen two rows in from the path. The children's deaths are recorded on the family stone, and from the dates given you can see that their deaths took place over a considerable number of years, suggesting that the term 'white plague' may also have been a general description for a variety of childhood diseases.

The existing church was built not long before Daniel Muir arrived in Dunbar, and was one of six churches in the town at the time. A re-developed site in Bamburgh Close was previously the site of Erskine Memorial Church, where Daniel Muir worshipped, but he was never content with the quality or quantity of his worship, complaining that his fellow Christians lacked 'zeal', always seeking some greater and more zealous way of expressing and sharing his convictions.

The six Dunbar churches were augmented by visiting missionaries and evangelists preaching to anyone who would listen, and by a variety of religious groups conducting revivals and open-air meetings of all kinds. It was to one of these groups that Daniel Muir was eventually drawn. They called themselves the Disciples of Christ and their evangelical call to arms was sounded in Scotland by the Gray brothers, although the sect originated in the Great Revival of the American frontier. Led by two Scottish immigrants to the New World, Thomas and Alexander Campbell, the group encouraged its adherants to go forth and spread the word, and to do so in the 'virgin land' of North America, creating what they saw as a new Eden in the wilderness. Their faith was personal, individual and homespun, with a literal adherance to the Bible and a disregard for established clerical channels.

This was just what Daniel Muir had been waiting, longing, hoping for, and at some stage in the autumn of 1848 he made up his mind to remove himself and his family to that new Eden across the Atlantic where he could raise his children in the simple, rustic way he chose, without interference from others, and preach the gospel as he saw fit. That decision was to change young John Muir's life immeasurably and to present him with the chance to immerse himself in the North American wilderness with which he would become identified.

Until February 1849 the young John knew nothing of his father's plans. Life for him was bounded by the daily routine of chores, meals, schoolwork, fist fights, scootchers, and the ever-present whippings from the schoolmaster and from his father. At home Daniel Muir required him to memorise entire sections of the Bible until by the age of eleven he knew 'about three fourths of the Old Testament and all of the New by heart and by sore flesh'. John Muir was later to comment ironically that these continual childhood whippings proved 'admirably influential in developing not only memory but fortitude as well'.

But his early life was not all beatings and learning by rote. In the long summer evenings when bedtime came before dark, he and his brother David would lie in bed

playing voyages around the world. Burrowing like moles, we visited France, India, America, and all the places we had ever heard of, our travels never ending until we fell asleep.

Checking on the two boys before she herself retired for the night, their mother would often have difficulty in finding them in the tangle of bedclothes, lying wherever sleep had overtaken them deep under the covers.

And there were the scootchers. A previous owner of the house, Dr Wightman, had left one of the upstairs rooms full of his laboratory equipment, and the Muirs, having no need for the room, left it just as it was, the chemical apparatus gathering dust and cobwebs. Servant girls whispered that the ghost of the departed doctor haunted the room, and one of the boys' greatest scootchers was to dare each other to enter it, running back in terror after a yard or less.

There was also a strong bond between John as the oldest boy of the family and his grandfather, David Gilrye, who lived nearby at 109-113 High Street. The house has been much altered since the Muirs' time, when Grandfather Gilrye lived there with his wife Margaret, their two servants Archibald and Sarah, and John's favourite aunt, Margaret Rae.

Some of John's earliest memories were those of his grandfather, who 'taught me my letters from shop signs across the street' and also helped the boy to read numbers and to tell the time by pointing to the numerals on the Town House clock. As you pass the Town House, with its Flemish tower and dialled clock, imagine the seventy year old David Gilrye accompanied by a little boy of three as they stand solemnly in front of the tower, concentrating on the numbers.

John Muir always remembered the early walks he took with his grandfather into the surrounding countryside where, one day, resting for a few minutes on a haycock, he heard 'a sharp, prickly,

> *Most people who are born into the world remain babies all their lives, their development being arrested like sun-dried seeds.*
>
> Letter written from Yosemite Valley to brother David, 1 March 1873

stinging cry'. Burrowing through the hay he discovered a mother field-mouse with her young. 'This to me was a wonderful discovery. No hunter could have been more excited on discovering a bear and her cubs in a wilderness den.'

The boys were forbidden by their father to wander away from the safety of the rear garden at the High Street house – he feared they would get into fights and bad company, and of course they did. As soon as they were able to climb over the high wall away they went, down to the rock pools on the seashore, or in the spring and summer up and up into the Lammermuirs, those beloved hills with their birds and burns and beeches, the soft spring rain stinging John's face or misting around him as he ran. Whenever he could escape from school or chores, or simply from his father's watchful eye, he ran in the Lammermuir Hills. Frederick Turner, in his excellent biography, *Rediscovering America: John Muir in His Time and Ours*, calls him the 'long-distance runner', so far and so regularly did he run. 'We thought nothing of running right ahead ten or a dozen miles before turning back; for we knew nothing about taking time by the sun and none of us had a watch in those days.'

And always at the end of such an escapade there was father, waiting with the switch. 'Late or early, the thrashing was sure, unless father happened to be away.'

John was no angel – writing his autobiography in maturity, he himself remarked 'so much like wild beasts are baby boys, little fighting, biting, climbing pagans'. He exhibited all the normal, anti-social behaviour of a young boy, including irritating his long-suffering sisters, who made no secret of their feelings about his non-stop chatter. As a child he gashed his tongue and was put to bed with a wad of cotton wool in his mouth. Falling asleep, he swallowed the wad and with it, as I imagined, my tongue also. My scream over so great a loss brought mother, and when she anxiously took me in her arms and inquired what was the matter, I told her that I had swallowed my tongue... My sisters, who were older than I, oftentimes said when I happened to be talking too much, 'It's a pity you hadn't swallowed at least half of that long tongue of yours when you were little.'

Despite such irritations, there was a closeness between the children which neither time nor distance diminished. In later years, when John was in funds and any of his brothers or sisters fell on hard times, he was there to help. In the early years, shortly after his brother David's birth, this 'help' took an unconventional form. The local doctor was vaccinating David, who was cradled in his mother's arms, and John saw blood on the baby's arm.

... unable to trust even my mother, I managed to spring up high enough to grab and bite the doctor's arm, yelling that I wasna gan to let him hurt my bonnie brither, while to my utter astonishment mother and the doctor only laughed at me.

Daniel Muir was not the only adult who thrashed the boys. School was a continual mixture of rote learning punctuated by whippings for transgressions against the master's rules, for failing to remember lessons, for being unruly, for fighting in the playground. The young John was sent to Davel Brae school at the tender age of three, where headmaster Mungo Siddons ruled with an iron hand and where John learned that to be a 'gude fechter' was the ambition of every boy. 'After attaining the manly, belligerent age of five or six years, very few of my schooldays passed without a fist fight, and half a dozen was no uncommon number.' The Scottish warriors William Wallace and Robert the Bruce were their boyhood heroes and 'of course we were all going to be soldiers'.

When, at the age of seven or eight, John Muir moved to the grammar school, ruled over by Dominie David Lyon, he had 'a terrible lot of fighting to do, because a new scholar had to meet every one of his age who dared to challenge him'. In addition to this, he would be whipped again at home if his father learned of the fights, and thrashed yet again by the Dominie for anything short of perfection in his studies.

There was nothing said about making the seats easy or the lessons easy. We were simply driven pointblank against our books like soldiers against the enemy, and sternly ordered, 'Up and at'em. Commit your lessons to memory!' If we failed in any part however slight, we were whipped; for the grand, simple, all-sufficing Scotch discovery had been made that there was a close connection between the skin and the memory, and that irritating the skin excited the memory to any required degree.

The site of the old grammar school has now been redeveloped and lies to the south-east of Dunbar's Logan Close, behind the old school wall. The crossroads at the end of Silver Street marked the boundary between rival groups of boys – the 'Streeties', sons of High Street businessmen and shopkeepers, and the 'Shories', whose fathers tended to be artisans and fisherman from the Dunbar waterfront – and these two opposing groups would engage in pitched battles on the Davel Brae or the seashore.

The physical endurance and ability to withstand pain which John Muir developed in these hard-won years before he reached the age of eleven were to remain with him throughout his life. Shivering with cold on a Californian mountain top, penniless and weak with hunger during his thousand mile walk through America's Deep South in the aftermath of the Civil War, he still retained a determination to go on, a sheer 'bloody-mindedness' which refused to give in to greater force.

Another result of his childhood experiences was to make him an opponent of violence – he later wrote movingly of the horrors and stupidity of war and removed himself to Canada rather than fight in the American Civil War – and to render him an opponent of prescribed ways of gathering knowledge, of ways of living his life. He found great pleasure in learning but he sat for no formal degree, preferring to seek his experiences in the 'university of life'. He was a lover of God but found inspiration and wonder in admiring God's works of nature in the wilderness rather than attaching himself to an organised church and worshipping indoors.

In maturity he was enormously aided by his ability to withstand cold, hunger and discomforts of many kinds which would have discouraged anyone raised in a kindlier atmosphere. In addition to the constant beatings and fistfights, his diet in those early years was plain and minimal, his father believing that anything more would have 'spoiled' the children. Breakfast was oatmeal porridge, the midday meal 'usually vegetable broth, a small piece of boiled mutton, and barley-meal scone'. After-school tea consisted of unbuttered bread (half a slice), more barley scone, and warm water to which a little milk and sugar was added – this insipid concoction going under the name of 'content', surely named by someone with a warped sense of humour. Before family worship and bed there would be a boiled potato and yet another helping of the ubiquitous barley scone. 'None of us liked the barley scone bread, therefore we got all we wanted of it, and in desperation had to eat it, for we were always hungry, about as hungry after as before meals.'

In the warmer weather while John was still an infant, cleanliness was ensured by salt water bathing, the servant girl stripping the children and plunging them into rock pools full of 'crawling crawfish and slippery wriggling snake-like eels'. After this terrifying experience it's not surprising that John did not teach himself to swim until his teenage years at the Wisconsin farm, but he retained a great fondness for the Firth of Forth and thought of his home shore whenever he caught a whiff of salt air, walking in the Florida backwoods or on the Californian coast.

Apart from the seashore and the Lammermuir Hills, the other boyhood memory which came often into Muir's mind in later years was that of Dunbar Castle. He learned to climb on its crumbling sandstone walls, which had weathered a thousand years by the time he first saw them. It lies in ruins now, many of its stones having being claimed by the North Sea and by the builders of early Dunbar. Today it's a peaceful place, with the seagulls swooping overhead, but in 1296 it was besieged by 'Longshanks', Edward I of England, and it is also to Dunbar Castle that his son, Edward II, retreated in 1314 after his defeat by the forces of Robert the Bruce at the Battle of Bannockburn, one of the greatest victories in Scottish history.

It was besieged yet again by an English army commanded by the Earl of Salisbury, against the defending forces of the Countess of Dunbar, 'Black Agnes' as she was known, a redoubtable woman who held out for five months against the invaders. Mary Queen of Scots sheltered there in March 1566 after the murder of her favourite servant, David Rizzio, and again in April 1567 with Lord Bothwell after yet another murder, that of her husband Lord Darnley at Kirk O'Field.

As he practised his climbing skills and as his friends dared him to climb higher and higher on the crumbling walls, John Muir would have been well aware of the violent past of the castle and the part it had played in Scottish history. Like William Wallace before him, he was fiercely proud of his heritage and of being a Scot. Even in his maturity, many years later in America, he never regarded himself as anything other than Scottish and took a special delight in the company and the humour of his fellow Scots.

But his future lay in the New World. On 1 February 1849, the High Street property was sold to Dr John Lorn, a local physician, the deed of sale was recorded on 12 February, and on the evening of 18 February the children were finally told. John and David were sitting in front of the fire in their grandparents' house, preparing their lessons as usual for the following day, when their father burst in with the news, '... the most wonderful, most glorious, that wild boys ever heard. 'Bairns', he said, 'you needna learn your lessons the nicht, for we're gan to America the morn!' '

The boys were delirious with happiness, thinking of all the Californian gold and birds' nests and trees full of sugar and wild places they would find in America, but their grandfather, deeply saddened at the loss of his daughter and grandchildren to an uncertain future in an unknown and distant land, warned them that not everything would be as they hoped across the other side of the Atlantic. 'Ah, poor laddies, poor laddies, you'll find something else ower the sea forbye gold and sugar, birds' nests and freedom fra lessons and schools. You'll find plenty hard, hard work.' And so we did'.

David Gilrye felt so strongly that his son-in-law was too unpredictable, too 'unworldly' to start from scratch in providing for his family in the 'virgin land' of the New World, that he forbade Daniel Muir to take the younger children and their mother to America until there was a suitable house built for them. And he was so opposed to the emigration that he removed Daniel from his will and left what he had to his daughter and the children. The rift between the two men was deep and bitter and lasted for the remainder of David Gilrye's life.

So Anne Gilrye Muir, her eldest daughter Margaret, and the younger children moved in with the grandparents across the High Street, and on the morning of 19 February 1849 Daniel left Dunbar with the two boys, John and David, and their thirteen year old sister Sarah. The reasons for Daniel Muir's decision – which he probably took alone, simply informing his dutiful wife when he saw fit – are not difficult to guess. He saw in the wilderness of America God's promised land in which he could build a new Eden, living and worshipping as he wanted, with his family removed from the 'temptations' of urban society. He was already much concerned over what he saw as the wildness of his two elder sons, the company they were keeping and their constant fistfights. All the thrashings he administered seemed to make little difference as long as the boys remained in that environment. Here was his opportunity to change all that, to give them a new start in a new land, and in addition to go forth and preach the gospel of the Disciples of Christ, to do what he regarded as God's work in bringing salvation to the unenlightened.

In 1848 the Californian Gold Rush was gathering momentum and Hector St. John de Crevecoeur's *Letters from an American Farmer*, first published in 1782, were enjoying renewed popularity. They depicted America as the promised land of opportunity, where a hardworking man could make a good life for himself and his family, untrammelled by the conditioning and restraints of the old world. For many people disillusioned with life back home, North America must indeed have beckoned as the land of opportunity. Crop failure and famine had dogged Scotland and England throughout 1847 and 1848, there was the threat of impending revolution in France and the fear that this might spread across the Channel. And the Highland Clearances which had started the previous century had from the 1820s onwards increased in their scope and ruthlessness. Families, evicted from their traditional lands to make way for sheep, saw little future for themselves in the new Scotland. It must have seemed to many people in the old country that their only hopes of success lay in the New World. Daniel Muir was one of them.

The four of them travelled by train to Glasgow – a journey which in itself must have caused great excitement to the children – and boarded the sailing ship on which Daniel Muir had booked passage. As the ship slipped her moorings and moved away down the Clyde the boys' joy must have reached unprecedented levels, and that happiness continued throughout the voyage, for on board there was no schooling, no lesson-learning, and very little parental supervision as their father suffered from seasickness much of the time. When he eventually rose from the prone position he was still not well enough to administer discipline, and sister Sarah never left her bunk the entire voyage. Left to their own devices, the delighted boys learned the rudiments of sailing, chattered to the captain and their fellow passengers and stayed on deck in the roughest Atlantic swell, untouched by any queasiness. In his auto-biography John Muir tells us this was his first experience of the power of the ocean, and in later years he would often insist on staying on deck in stormy weather, delighting in the wildness when his fellow passengers were clutching their stomachs below.

For John and David the passage was a six week holiday, despite the fact that the ship rolled like a drunken sailor and was poorly equipped for the many emigrants it carried. At this time of massive emigration to North America, conditions on board the emigrant ships were often appalling – overcrowded accommodation below decks, bad water and constant outbreaks of disease in the unsanitary conditions, particularly in rough weather. Typhus, dysentery and cholera were common, and there was sickness on the Muir's ship, although Muir in his account gives no indication of any deaths on board.

Many of the emigrants were bound for Scottish settlements in Nova Scotia and Ontario in Canada, or the Carolinas and Virginia. Daniel Muir had originally intended to settle in Canada but during the voyage he heard stories of the back-breaking toil required of a man to clear the heavily forested Canadian soil. He decided instead to head for the open prairies of the American mid-west, and when he discovered from fellow Disciples of Christ on board that he would find like-minded settlers in Wisconsin he determined that Wisconsin was the place for him.

On 5 April 1849 the Muirs disembarked through the quarantine station in New York harbour. John Muir's life in the New World had begun.

CHAPTER 2

'Oh, that glorious Wisconsin wilderness.'

The family travelled first to Milwaukee in Michigan and then continued their 'wavering way westward' on the cart of a farmer who agreed to carry them and their heavy luggage the hundred miles into Wisconsin. Daniel Muir left his three children with neighbours for several days while he found suitable land and while he and the neighbours built a small shanty.

> To this charming hut, in the sunny woods, overlooking a flowery glacier meadow and a lake rimmed with white water-lilies, we were hauled by an ox-team across trackless carex swamps and low rolling hills sparely dotted with round-headed oaks.

John and David couldn't wait until the cart came to a halt. Spotting a blue jay's nest, they leaped to the ground and were already up the tree before the others reached the shanty. This enthusiasm for the wildlife of Fountain Lake Farm, as Daniel named it, was to stay with John all his life. His father had chosen an area of poor soil which would soon be exhausted, but the beauty of the lake and its abundance of plants, birds and animals enchanted him.

> This sudden plash into pure wilderness – baptism in nature's warm heart – how utterly happy it made us! Nature streaming into us, wooingly teaching her wonderful glowing lessons, so unlike the dismal grammar ashes and cinders so long thrashed into us.

All around him were ...

> blue jays, nighthawks, whip-poor-whills, woodpeckers, brown thrushes, kingbirds, hen-hawks, song sparrows, bluebirds. Lightning bugs put on their spectacular show in the meadow below the farm, partridges drummed their wings, frogs sang their love songs, 'Isaac, Isaac; Yacob, Yacob; Israel, Israel; shouted in sharp, ringing, far-reaching tones, as if they had all been to school and severely drilled in elocution.

The family cat dragged in a variety of strange small animals, there was the occasional rattlesnake, copperheads and puff snakes, Canada geese flying overhead and loons arriving in the spring. In the harsh winters the thermometer plummeted to twenty or thirty degrees below zero, the lake froze over and snow blanketed the landscape for months. In his autobiography, *The Story of My Boyhood and Youth*, Muir talks of neighbours' frost-damaged 'feet, ears and fingers'. In the summers there were great thunder storms, heat, humidity, and the ever-present deer-flies and mosquitoes with '... their enthusiastic appreciation of boys full of lively red blood, and of girls in full bloom fresh from cool Scotland or England'.

But most important of all, there was the lake, in which the young Muir taught himself to swim, almost drowning in the process, and where he got his 'finest lessons and sermons from the water and flowers, ducks, fishes and muskrats'. So deep was his love for Fountain Lake and its water meadows that he spent the rest of his life trying to purchase it, to keep it the way he found it.

> I want to keep it untrampled for the sake of its ferns and flowers; and even if I should never see it again, the beauty of its lilies and orchids are so pressed into my mind I shall always enjoy looking back at them in imagination, even across seas and continents, and perhaps after I am dead.

Muir never succeeded in purchasing the lake, but in May 1957 forty acres of the lake area were dedicated as the Muir Memorial County Park, which has now grown to include the lakeside meadows. You can see John Muir's lilies and frogs and lightning bugs by visiting the park. Whether you're travelling from Minneapolis, Minnesota or from Madison in Wisconsin, take Interstate 90/94 to Portage, Wisconsin. From Minneapolis, take the State Highway 33 exit to Portage, and from Madison exit on US Highway 51 north. Once you reach State Highway 33, drive eastwards through Portage, turning left (north) just east of Portage on County Road F.

Continue driving for approximately ten miles until you see Muir Memorial Park on your right, with a plaque about Muir standing near the county road. You can drive down almost to the water's edge and gaze at the lake view

Everybody needs beauty as well as bread.

The Yosemite, 1912

which enchanted Muir when he first arrived as an eleven year old boy. There's a trail which takes you around the edge of the lake, where in the warm weather you can also share the *real* John Muir experience of close encounters with the local mosquito population.

On the far side of the water is where the original Fountain Lake Farm stood – long since demolished – on a knoll looking down over sloping meadows to the water's edge. Scottish settlers traditionally built their houses on higher ground, and the Muirs were no exception. The site, now part of the Fountain Lake Farm National Historic Landmark, is owned by an ecologist and landscape architect who is gradually returning the meadows to the way they were when the young John Muir arrived in 1849. The land has been cleared of pine trees and resown with prairie grasses, bobwhite quail have been reintroduced, and clearcutting of vegetation has restored many of the views which Muir so loved. 'This is the first place', says the owner, 'that any American conceived the notion of preserving nature for its own sake. We're used to thinking of historical significance in terms of architecture – Victorians and Queen Annes. Here, it's the living ingredients of the landscape that are important.'

The idea of formally designating Fountain Lake a protected area was suggested by conservationist Aldo Leopold in 1948. His *Sand County Almanac* is an ode to the intrinsic beauty and worth of the land and its creatures, and a plea to men to stop messing about with them. Like Muir, he could not understand how humans can delude themselves that they are separate from the 'outdoors', somehow above and beyond it. Leopold's land ethic 'changes the role of homo sapiens from conqueror of the land-community to plain member and citizen of it'. Like Muir, Leopold spoke out against the distancing of many people from the natural world.

Commemorative plaque

'There are two dangers in not owning a farm. One is the danger of supposing that breakfast comes from the grocery, and the other that heat comes from the furnace.'

Aldo Leopold's now famous Shack lies in Wisconsin's sand country, around thirty miles west of Fountain Lake Farm, and like the Muirs' farm its soil is agriculturally poor and easily worn out. Leopold is rightfully regarded as a worthy successor to John Muir, and you can visit the Aldo Leopold Foundation and the 1,400 acre Leopold Memorial Reserve at Levee Road, Baraboo. Contact them first for an appointment (Tel. 608 355 0279, Fax. 608 356 7309).

The Shack was just a chicken coop on worn out land when Leopold acquired it, and his five children wondered what on earth their father was thinking of. Rebuilt by the Leopold family in the thirties, it is now the one-and-only chicken coop to be found on the National Register of Historic Places. With its simplicity and lack of modern conveniences, the Shack has become a symbol for living lightly on the land, for promoting a healthy and respectful land-human relationship. Try to find time to read at least a little of *Sand County Almanac*. It will give you a greater understanding of the land in which John Muir grew to manhood, the ways in which the Wisconsin sand country entered his blood and created the foundation for his lifelong love affair with the wilderness.

Muir tells us in his autobiography that it was at Fountain Lake

Aldo Leopold's Shack in Wisconsin's Sand Country

he first became convinced that all living things are intimately con-
nected, that animals are not inferior beasts created for human use.
The family pig comes rushing home minus one of her piglets and
Muir says that he can never forget

> the solemn awe and fear in the eyes of that old mother ... it was as
> unmistakable and deadly a fear as I ever saw expressed by any human
> eye, and corroborates in no uncertain way the oneness of us all. Surely
> a better time must be drawing nigh when godlike human beings will
> become truly humane, and learn to put their animal fellow mortals in
> their hearts instead of on their backs or in their dinners.

He tells the story of Watch, the dog who is 'condemned and
executed' by Daniel Muir

> because his taste for chickens was too much like our own. None of our
> fellow mortals is safe who eats what we eat, who in any way interferes
> with our pleasures, or who may be used for work or food, clothing or
> ornament, or mere cruel, sportish amusement.

But perhaps the most heart-rending story of the autobiography
is Daniel Muir's treatment of Nob, the family's much-loved work-
horse. In Wisconsin, Daniel Muir delighted in attending every
available religious meeting, preaching at many of them, and, in
haste to return to a meeting from nearby Portage one summer's,
day Daniel drove Nob too hard. 'I shall never forget how tired and
wilted she looked that evening when I unhitched her; how she
drooped in her stall, too tired to eat or even to lie down.' As a
result of Daniel's uncaring treatment, Nob dies, 'bleeding and
gasping for breath'. Muir's resulting hatred for the misuse of animals never falters – in maturity, in his California orchards, he had
a reputation for dismissing on the spot any worker discovered
maltreating the farm horses – and he denounces

> the teachings of churches and schools, where too often the mean,
> blinding, loveless doctrine is taught that animals have neither mind nor
> soul, have no rights that we are bound to respect, and were made only
> for man, to be petted, spoiled, slaughtered, or enslaved.

If Daniel Muir's religious fervour had not diminished in the
New World, nor had his zeal for beating his sons. Muir tells us

drily that most of the beatings 'were outrageously severe, and utterly barren of fun'. *The Story of My Boyhood and Youth* was written in Muir's mature years and shocked many readers when it was first published in serial form. William Frederic Badè, Muir's literary executor and compiler of *The Life and Letters of John Muir*, suggests that while many autobiographers edit out family discord, Muir chose to include it in the hope of persuading parents to rear their children without chastising them, particularly in the name of religion.

> When the rod is falling on the flesh of a child, and what may oftentimes be worse, heartbreaking scolding falling on its tender little heart, it makes the whole family seem far from the Kingdom of Heaven. In all the world I know of nothing more pathetic and deplorable than a broken-hearted child, sobbing itself to sleep after being unjustly punished by a truly pious and conscientious misguided parent.

There is a major contrast between John Muir's upbringing and the way in which he raised his own two daughters, doting on them, spending hours telling them stories and introducing them to plants, asking the girls how they would like it if the plants didn't know *their* names.

Beatings were not the only hardship facing the Muir children. Soon John and David's joyous explorations of Fountain Lake were curtailed by the hard labour of clearing the land. For them there was no more schooling, for Daniel Muir put them to work. Apart from Sundays, which were mainly spent in worship, from now on they had only two days holiday a year, the fourth of July and New Year's Day.

A fine frame house was constructed on a knoll overlooking the lake, and in November 1849 John's mother Anne and the remainder of the Muir children arrived from Dunbar. From that date until he left home at the age of twenty two, John, being the eldest boy, bore the

Fountain Lake Farm

brunt of the farm workload. 'I was put to the plough at the age of twelve, when my head reached but little above the handles, and for many years I had to do the greater part of the ploughing. It was hard work for so small a boy ... .'

Looking back on those early days at Fountain Lake, Muir bitterly regretted the 'vice of over-industry' which drove many of the Scottish settlers to labour such long hours on the land. For him, seventeen hour long days were the norm 'while I was only a small stunted boy', and he was known as the runt of the family because of the way in which such intensive labour delayed his teenage growth. 'Men and boys, and in those days even women and girls, were cut down while cutting the wheat.' His sister Sarah never fully regained her health and John himself was plagued for the remainder of his life by a recurring cough and by bouts of pneumonia. One year he had mumps during harvest time. Daniel Muir refused to let him leave the fields. The only respite was when he went down with pneumonia, although 'no physician was called, for father was an enthusiast, and always said and believed that God and hard work were by far the best doctors'.

Muir makes a distinction between the American farmers, 'wisely content with smaller fields and less of everything', and the work ethic of the new settlers from Scotland who could not rest if there was an 'uncut weed' on their farm. He also deplores his father's attitude in making a virtue of suffering. In an area where fallen wood was plentiful – slow burning oak and hickory were readily available on the farm – Daniel Muir allowed no fire in the house except for the kitchen stove, around which the entire family huddled in sub-zero temperatures, boots and socks freezing overnight under the tiny stove.

Man has injured every animal he has touched.

Journal entry,
11 February 1869

After eight years of what John Muir describes as 'drudgery' at Fountain Lake Farm, the soil was exhausted. Tree clearing to the north had lowered the water table, and as Linnie Marsh Wolfe points out in her biography of Muir, 'they had felled the trees that homed the birds that would have eaten the larvae that grew into bugs that ate the wheat'. Wheat was no longer a viable crop at Fountain Lake, and so Daniel Muir bought a half-section of land six miles to the south-east of the original farm. He called it Hickory Hill Farm, and it stands there today, although the original timber building has been clad with brick. It lies on the outskirts of the town of Buffalo in Marquette County and is still a working farm in private ownership.

To John Muir the move meant starting yet again on the backbreaking work of tree-clearing and ploughing, Muir Senior being too preoccupied with saving souls and bible study to give much time to the farm work.

The soil there was better but the farm had no 'living water', so Daniel ordered John to dig a well. After the first ten feet, John struck sandstone. Blasting was tried unsuccessfully, and Daniel gave his son the task of chipping out the well by hand, using a hammer and chisel in a space only three feet in diameter. John laboured away at his task for 'weeks and months' until the 'dreary bore' was around eighty feet deep, until one day he started to lose consciousness from the affects of chokedamp – carbonic acid gas which had gathered in the well-bottom. His father managed to haul him up in time, but it was a near thing. Within a couple of days, having been advised how to dispel choke-damp, Daniel ordered his son back down the well. In his autobiography John Muir comments bitterly 'Constant dropping wears away stone. So does constant chipping, while at the same time wearing away the chipper. Father never spent an hour in that well'.

Hickory Hill Farm

John did eventually strike water, at ninety feet, and the well is still standing today in the farmyard at Hickory Hill. So too is the barn which the Muirs erected, with its untrimmed timbers and rafters just as they were when John Muir fashioned them. Earlier this century the entire barn was raised hydraulically and placed on a stone foundation, with the original structure undisturbed.

The Hickory Hill Barn built by the Muirs

Life at Hickory Hill was no more comfortable than it had been at Fountain Lake. Many years later, John's younger brother David wrote,

John, do you remember our bedroom at Hickory Hill on the north side – never smelt fire or sun, window none too tight, three in a bed, Dan in the middle, and quilts frozen about our faces in the morning, and how awful cold it was to get up ... and dress and go down to the kitchen barefooted? Oo-oo-ooo, it makes me shiver to think of it.

Without the stimulus of formal schooling, the young Muir longed for books, strictly forbidden by his father who viewed the Bible as the only book anyone could ever need. Friendly neighbours lent him the classics and he hid them from Daniel Muir, reading avidly in any spare moment he could find. Irritated at finding his son yet again with his nose in a book at bedtime, Daniel incautiously told John, 'If you will read, get up in the morning and read. You may get up in the morning as early as you like.'

From then on John rose at one in the morning, but knowing his father would begrudge the wood for a fire, kept himself warm by physical activity instead of reading. Working in the cellar, he first of all designed and constructed a self-setting sawmill, followed by 'water-wheels, curious doorlocks and latches, thermometers, hygrometers, pyrometers, clocks, a barometer, an automatic contrivance for feeding the horses at any required hour, a lamp-lighter and fire-lighter, an early-or-late-rising machine ...'. Daniel Muir, gritting his teeth at the noise emanating from the cellar, but as a man of principle unwilling to go back on a promise given, must have been doubly irritated by the fact that John's workbench lay directly underneath his father's study-bedroom. Poetic justice, perhaps?

Eventually, at the ripe old age of twenty two and motivated by a neighbour's suggestion that the young man should exhibit some of his inventions at the State Fair in Madison, Muir finally decided to fly the nest. Packing up two of his inventions, a clockpiece and the early-rising machine, he said his farewells with only fifteen dollars in his pocket, his father having refused him any aid.

Despite Daniel Muir's belief that his son would find the world an unkind place, John 'found no lack of kindness and sympathy'. In Pardeeville, from where he caught the train to Madison, his inventions attracted an interested group of bystanders, all trying to guess what the machines might do. And in the Fine Arts Hall of the State Fair his clock and early-rising machine were highlights of the show. For the first time John Muir's name appeared in print, in the Wisconsin State Journal of 25 September 1860. Under the title 'An Ingenious Whittler' appeared the following report:

> While at the Fair Grounds this morning we saw some very ingenious specimens of mechanism, in the form of clocks, made by Mr John Muir, of Buffalo, Marquette County. They were without cases, and were whittled out of pine wood. The wheels moved with beautiful evenness. One registered not only hours but minutes, seconds, and days of the month. The other was in the shape of a scythe, the wheels being arranged along the part representing the blade. It was hung in a dwarf burr oak very tastefully ornamented with moss about its roots. We will venture to predict that few articles will attract as much attention as these products of Mr Muir's ingenuity.

Following his success at the State Fair, Muir received a number of job offers. He chose one from an inventor by the name of Norman Wiard, agreeing to work in his machine shop in return for training. Wiard was the inventor of the Lady Franklin, a flat-bottomed steamboat which he claimed would run on ice and thus

Surely a better time must be drawing nigh when godlike human beings will become truly humane, and learn to put their animal fellow mortals in their hearts instead of on their backs or in their dinners.

A Thousand Mile Walk
to the Gulf, 1916

revolutionise winter travel on the northern rivers.

Muir returned with Wiard to Prairie du Chien where the Lady Franklin proved unsuccessful in her ice trials and her inventor was discredited. John decided to return to Madison, but in the meantime he had established a friendship with the Pelton family who operated the Mondell House Hotel in Prairie du Chien. His friendship with Emily Pelton, niece of the family, would remain close for the remainder of his life, and many of the glimpses which we have today into Muir's later life come from his frequent letters to Emily.

The Peltons were 'society' to John the farm boy, and when he gleefully wrote to his mother about their social gatherings, Anne Muir persuaded her husband that John needed better clothes than the rough homespun in which he had left home. Uncharacteristically, Daniel Muir sent his son a suit of 'boughten clothes' and a trunk to put them in, a sign that there was perhaps some understanding of worldly needs beyond those of bible study.

Back in Madison, John worked at a variety of jobs while longing to become a student at the fledgling University of Wisconsin. Despite the fact that since leaving Scotland at the age of eleven he had received almost no formal schooling, he eventually plucked up the courage in 1861 to request admission and was accepted. Dazed with happiness at his good fortune, over a two and a half year period he studied a range of subjects – Greek, Latin, geology, mathematics, physics.

It was in Madison that he established a friendship with Jeanne Carr that would profoundly influence his life. Mrs Carr was the wife of one of his teachers, Ezra Slocum Carr, a professor of chemistry and natural history. The young student became a frequent visitor to their house, and Jeanne Carr, an intellectual and a botanist, introduced Muir to many of the new ideas of the time. Throughout his life, she continued to act as his mentor and to send him men and women she felt he should meet. It was Jeanne Carr who sent Ralph Waldo Emerson to him in Yosemite, and it was Jeanne Carr who introduced him to Louie Strentzel, the woman who later became his wife.

You can still see the handsome Madison house in which the Carrs lived at 114 West Gilman Street, and visit the University buildings in which Muir worked during his two and a half years in the city. His rooms, on the second storey of North Hall, became a magnet for students and faculty as his inventions multiplied and his local fame grew. He designed and built a bed which shot the sleeper upright at a pre-set time, a 'loafer's chair' which ejected the unsuspecting sitter, and a study desk. This tall desk incorporated a timing device which produced books at set intervals, replacing them when the next volume was needed. The nine-foot high desk now stands in a glass case in the foyer of the State Historical Society of Wisconsin, 816 State Street, on the University campus. Looking at it, its intricate design of wheels and cogs, constructed with very little in the way of mechanical tools, you can see why many of Muir's fellow students regarded him as a genius.

Under the tutelage of Ezra Carr, he studied the subject of glaciation and the ideas of Louis Agassiz, the Swiss glaciologist, who believed that the 'universal ice sheet' of an earlier Ice Age was responsible for the formation and shape of many contemporary landforms. Muir's later glacial studies in Yosemite were very much influenced by what he learned at Madison.

Another man who had a profound influence on the young Muir was Increase A. Lapham, who preached against the folly of tree destruction in Wisconsin, telling his listeners of the perils of deforestation. At Fountain Lake Farm Muir had seen for himself the results of excessive clearance, and in later years he would take up the cause of forest preservation.

Influential too was Dr James Davie Butler, a Classics scholar and admirer of Emerson, who taught Muir the value of recording his thoughts in his own way, his own language. When in later years Muir moved from formal delivery to find his own voice, his straightforward, informal style owed much to the early encouragement of Butler. And it was at this time that he became accustomed to keeping a journal, a record of thoughts and findings from which we are able to learn so much about Muir's journeys, both internal and external.

He had always had an interest in plants but it was a fellow student, Milton Griswold, who made Muir realise that botany was a subject in which he could completely immerse himself. From the moment Griswold pointed out that the locust tree and the pea plant hailed from the same family, Muir was hooked, and he remained so for the rest of his life, 'botanising' at every available opportunity.

While studying he continued working at various jobs which would feed and clothe him – one winter he taught at a school ten miles south of Madison, and in the summer he helped with the harvest at Hickory Hill. But, like his fellow students, he could not ignore the growing antipathy between the north and south, and in April 1861, at Fort Sumter, the first shots of the Civil War were fired. Many of his friends enlisted and the State Fair Grounds became Camp Randall, where recruits were drilled and where later on in the war too many of them came home to die of their wounds.

John Muir's study desk

John was restless and unhappy, opposed to the war and uncertain which way to turn. In the spring of 1863, he talked to his professors about studying medicine in Michigan, then changed his mind. In March the Enrollment Act called for the drafting of all eligible males between the ages of twenty and forty five, and in New York there were draft riots, with negroes mutilated and killed. With two student friends, Rice and Blake, he took a botanical trip on the Wisconsin River, and in July of that year worked on the harvest at Fountain Lake. He was twenty five years old. His brother Dan had already 'skedaddled' to Canada to escape the draft, at his mother's bequest, but still John hesitated. In early March 1864, he hesitated no longer. He would wander away 'happy and free, poor and rich'. He would go to Canada.

CHAPTER 3

Canada

WHEN MUIR CROSSED INTO Canada in March 1864 – probably via Michigan and Sault St Marie – the Civil War was still raging. President Abraham Lincoln, however, was not totally preoccupied with thoughts of battle, for in 1864 he signed over Yosemite Valley and the Mariposa Big Tree Grove to the state of California. Both areas were created state parks – the nation's first act of wilderness preservation.

Whether the Lincoln presidency would have gone on to create many more such parks nobody knows, for the following year, as every American schoolchild can tell you, Honest Abe was assassinated by John Wilkes Booth while attending a performance of 'Our American Cousin' at Ford's Theatre in Washington DC. John Muir's thoughts on the continuing slaughter on the battle-fields and in Ford's Theatre are unknown, as no journal of his Canadian sojourn survives. Either he didn't keep one or it went up in flames when the mill in which he was working burned to the ground. The information we have today is gleaned from a few autobiographical fragments and from letters to his friends, many of them written well after his Canadian years.

Nor can we be sure exactly why Muir decided on Canada. One obvious reason is that he didn't wish to fight against the South, having very little sympathy for violence of any kind. At university in Madison he had expressed great shock and sorrow at the outbreak of war, and the religion in which he had been raised preached personal rather than collective responsibility. All the information we have from his journals, letters, and published work confirms his opposition to military conflict, and there is always, of course, the normal drive for self-preservation. Many of the young men who had left Camp Randall with high spirits and a belief in fighting for their country, had not returned, or had returned terribly damaged. Why would Muir wish to suffer the same fate? His brother Dan was already in Canada, and John, also, was eager to explore the bogs and wilderness of the sparsely populated areas to the north of Wisconsin.

Whatever the reasons, Canada it was. It is difficult to tell exactly where he wandered, as the only record of his travels is gleaned from the notes and dates attached to his plant collection, later deposited in the safe keeping of Julia Merrill Moores of Indianapolis. The plant identification slips show that in March he visited the islands and northern shores of Ontario's Georgian Bay, on Lake Huron. In May he was in south eastern Grey County, in June and July exploring the Holland River swamps, followed by a visit to Niagara Falls and a meeting with his brother Dan in September.

Somewhere along the way, in the midst of a vast tamarac and arbor-vitae swamp, he came upon one of the most elusive of plants, *Calypso Borealis* or the Hider of the North.

> I found Calypso on the mossy bank of a stream, growing not in the ground but on a bed of yellow mosses in which its small white bulb had found a soft nest and from which its one leaf and one flower sprung. ... no other bloom was near it, for the bog a short distance below the surface was still frozen, and the water was ice cold. It seemed the most spiritual of all the flower people I had ever met. I sat down beside it and fairly cried for joy.

Muir's use of the phrase 'flower people' in indicative of the way in which he regarded plants as friends, as possessed of character and individual traits.

The month in which he found *Calypso* is hotly disputed by Muir scholars, but from his description of the frozen bog and the ice-cold water it is probable that it was in late May or early June – cold enough for ice but warm enough for the plant to bloom in a sheltered spot. The importance of the discovery lies in the effect it had on Muir.

> This Calypso meeting happened some forty-five years ago, and it was more memorable and impressive than any of my meetings with human beings excepting, perhaps, Emerson and one or two others.

Profoundly moved by the experience, he wrote of it in glowing terms to one of his former professors, James Butler, who had the letter published in *The Boston Recorder*, the first time Muir's writing appeared in print.

Unsure whether his name had come up in the draft list back home and whether he might be turned in as a deserter, Muir for the most part kept well away from towns. With his strong Scottish accent, it was easy for him to be accepted as a new Canadian. In the backwoods he came across a number of recent settlers, many of them from Scotland, and bemoaned the way in which they were felling the 'beautiful trees'.

He didn't think too much of Canadians either,

> hard-working, hard drinking, stolid Canadians. In vain is the glorious chart of God in Nature spread out for them. So many acres chopped is their motto, so they grub away amid the smoke of magnificent forest trees, black as demons and material as the soil they move upon.

He stayed a month with the Campbells, a Scottish family, and was appalled to hear the stories of how many Highlanders had been driven from their homes by landowners, such as the Duke of Sutherland, to make room for sheep.

Meeting up with Dan and discussing where to hole up for the hard Canadian winter, he heard from his brother of the Trout family of Meaford, on the shores of Georgian Bay. Dan had worked in the Trouts' sawmill the previous year and felt sure there would be winter work there for the two of them. Many years later, William Henry Trout put together a *Trout Family History*, published in 1916, in which he describes with pleasure the year and a half which the Muirs spent at the mill. And as for John, he fell in love with the area.

The clearest way into the Universe is through a forest wilderness.

Journal entry written during a sled trip to the Muir Glacier, Alaska, July 1890

When I came to the Georgian Bay of Lake Huron, whose waters are so transparent and beautiful, and the forests about its shores with their ferny, mossy dells and deposits of boulder clay, it seemed to be a most favourable place for study.... . In a beautiful dell, only a mile or two from the magnificent bay, I fortunately found work in a factory where there was a sawmill and lathes for turning out rake, broom, and fork handles.

At the time of the Muirs' arrival in Meaford in late 1864, the settlement's population was 1,100 souls; it could boast four hotels and a daily steamer connection with the railhead at Collingwood, weather and ice permitting. The town lies on the beautiful Georgian Bay of Lake Huron, a little over 150 kilometres north west of Toronto, and is approached from the east and the west by Highway 26, which runs along the southern curve of Georgian Bay. Coming from Toronto, take Highway 400 north to Midhurst, just north of Barrie, then Highway 26 west all the way into Meaford. If you enter Canada from the United States via the Sault Sainte Marie crossing, following the route that John Muir probably took, take Highway 17 east alongside the North Channel of Georgian Bay to just south-west of the town of Sudbury. At Sudbury turn south-east on Highway 69 to drive all the way down the eastern shores of the Bay until you reach Barrie and connect with Highway 26. The drive is over 650 kilometres long, with thousands of tiny islands lying just off the coast – a naturalist's and walker's paradise, which must have delighted John Muir if he did indeed travel this route.

In mid 1865 Dan returned to the United States, but John stayed on at Trout Hollow, completing a contract which he had signed with the Trouts to 'make one thousand dozen rakes and turn thirty thousand broom handles'. With his inherent mechanical ability, he revolutionised the factory, designing a self-acting lathe and a number of devices for speeding up rake production. On the banks of the Big Head River, close to the sawmill-factory, he shared a small cabin with the junior Trouts, William and Peter, and with Trout business partner Charles Jay. Mary, William's sister, acted as their housekeeper, and there were frequent visits from a younger sister, Hattie, whom John described as

> a very happy and sportive fish who employs herself in giggling and making giggle for hours at a time ... about twenty years of age, five and a half feet long and will perhaps sometime join affinity to the Jay who whistles and coos and gesticulates so funnily to her.

Hattie certainly liked to spend as much time as possible at the cabin, and a number of commentators have suggested that she had a special affection for John rather than Charles Jay. John's letter to her from Indianapolis in January 1867 intimates that from his viewpoint their relationship was friendly rather than romantic. 'What you say upon friendship is all true, and I believe it all, I confess Hattie, that the deep substantial warmth of your feelings a little surprises me and I never thought to find in you so true a friend ...'

The group of young people became firm friends, loved to tease each other and spent hours in discussion. They appeared to have a considerable admiration for Muir's intellect – in his family history, William Trout comments that with John Muir amongst them 'our log house in the mill hollow might modestly claim the same dignity as a university', although it should be noted that this history was written *after* Muir achieved fame and fortune. Perhaps his friends weren't quite so complimentary at the time and were more inclined to tease him about his non-stop talking (his sisters frequently remarked on this too) or about the 'cat' incident. John was forever admonishing them about killing insects, saying bugs have as much right to life as we do, until one day, attempting to remove a bird from the cat's mouth

> she would not let it go, and I choked her and choked her to make her let it go until I choked her to death, though I did not mean to, and they both lay dead upon the floor. I waited to see if she would not receive back one of her nine lives, but to my grief I found that I had taken them all, so I buried her beside some cucumber vines in the garden. When the rest came home I told what had occurred, and Charley Jay, who is as full of wit and

The Trout Hollow Cabin

jokes as the pond was of cold water one night, said 'Now John is always
scolding us about killing spiders and flies but when we are away he chokes
the cats', and they kept saying 'poor kitty', 'poor puss', for weeks afterwards to make me laugh.

One of their favourite discussion topics was religion. Darwin's
Origin of the Species had appeared in 1859 and had given rise to
heated debate. The Trouts and the Jays were members of the
Disciples of Christ church and John of course had been raised in
the same faith. But by this time he was already beginning to question the rightness of any religion which defined man as the centre
of the universe and relegated all other living things to the status of
human-fodder – a topic on which he was to concentrate during his
subsequent thousand mile walk to the Gulf of Mexico. And he
wrote to Jeanne Carr that he preferred to worship outdoors,
where he could see God's hand in the beauty of nature, rather than
within the four walls of a church.

His faith in God, however, was strong. William Trout recalls
that

Though ardently devoted to science, as well as the study of nature, yet
the agnostic tendencies that had their beginning about that time found
no sympathy with him. With him there was no dark chilly reasoning
that chance and the survival of the fittest accounted for all things.

It would hardly have been surprising if Daniel Muir's narrow
interpretation of religion – and in particular his personal version
of the Disciples of Christ faith – had turned
John against his maker, but there's very little
evidence that anything of the kind occurred.
He didn't always agree with the ways in
which men regulated their religion, he didn't
want to be organised and structured, told
how or when to worship, but his writings are
full of the God that he saw in the natural
world.

Whether or not Muir was a regular
attendee at Disciples of Christ meetings in
Meaford it is difficult to tell. The church jour-

*Only spread
a fern-frond
over a man's
head and
worldly cares
are cast out...*

My First Summer in
the Sierra, 1911

nals compiled by Disciples David Layton and Charles Jay don't mention his name, but given that his stay in Trout Hollow was relatively short, this is not surprising. In letters to Emily Pelton and to his sisters he mentions 'going to church'. Frederic William Badè has him teaching Sunday School in Meaford and 'leaving some of his books to his Sunday School class of admiring boys', but again the church records show no sign of this.

The Meaford Disciples church in Nelson Street, which Muir may or may not have attended each week, was built between 1854 and 1858, the first one in the town. In 1887 it was deconsecrated and sold, and it now houses the Back Street Café. Outside, it still resembles fairly closely the way it was in the 1860s; inside, it serves mouth-watering seafood crêpes and fresh salmon sandwiches where the Disciples used to congregate.

The new Disciples church, now known as the Church of Christ, is just up the road at 113 Nelson Street and still adheres to most of the Disciples' principles of John Muir's day. There are, for instance, no pictures or ornaments, and no piano or organ on the premises, the music being provided by the congregation's voices. Baptism is by immersion and one of the basic tenets of the church is constant scriptural reference, reading the New Testament as a guideline for everyday living – fundamentalism, as it's often called. Males are regarded as the spiritual heads of families and women are not authorised to speak out in formal church services. Church structure and practice has not changed much since John Muir's time. Interested visitors are welcome, and by visiting the church you can achieve something of an understanding of the beliefs in which he was reared.

The former Meaford Disciples of Christ Church which John Muir attended during his stay at Trout Hollow

Not that Daniel Muir was representative of Disciple behaviour, certainly not in the way he whipped and worked his children, denying them free expression of their talents. Understandably, Daniel Muir has been given a bad press by most of the Muir biographers, and some of that bad press has rubbed off over the years on the Disciples of Christ. This is unfair, for three reasons.

Firstly, each Disciples church, and the individuals within it, chooses its own method of operating and has a considerable degree of autonomy over day-to-day affairs, with the result that no two churches are identical. As an individual member of the Disciples, Daniel Muir preached wherever people would listen to him, and he was no more representative of his church than any other Disciple of his time.

Secondly, even at a time of evangelical teaching and religious revivals, Daniel was an extremist in everything he did. He was an over-zealous – some would say fanatical – worshipper, and in the same way he overdid fatherhood, pushing his children to impossible lengths in an attempt, as he saw it, to save their souls.

Thirdly, appallingly cruel and unreasonable though he seems to us today in the treatment of his children – particularly of John – he was not that unusual in the Scotland of his day, where violence was a way of life. At school in Dunbar, the young John was beaten regularly by his teachers and by his fellow pupils, not just by his father. Life had been hard for Daniel Muir and he made it equally hard for his own children. It was only in old age, living with his youngest daughter Joanna and her family, that he accepted how uncompromising, unfair and unkind he had been. Being representative of hardline men of his time does not, of course, excuse his behaviour. It is, however, incorrect to connect such behaviour with the Disciples, who did not beat their children any more, or any less, than non-Disciple parents.

On the cold windy night of 21 February 1866, the cedar shake roof of the Trout mill caught alight, possibly ignited by sparks from the nearby cabin chimney. The mill burned to the ground, and along with it Muir's notebooks and his investment in all those rakes and broom handles. There was no insurance, no money to pay him for his work, so he took an IOU for his share, bade his friends goodbye and again moved on.

The Trout family subsequently dispersed, the land passed into other hands, and that would probably have been the end of it for those on the trail of John Muir in Canada, had it not been for a donation, a rediscovery and a great deal of detective work. In 1994, Harriet Trout's grandaughter, Marion (Dow) Dean, donated to Meaford Museum five letters which had been written by John Muir to his friends in Meaford. The letters sat in the safe until 1997 when their historical value was assessed and they were made public. Dated July 1866 to January 1870, they throw new light on Muir's subsequent stay in Indianapolis, and on his sojourn at Trout Hollow, in particular Hattie's affection for Muir.

I care to live only to entice people to look at Nature's loveliness.

Letter written from Yosemite Valley to Jeanne Carr, 7 October 1874

The letters provided the impulse for several people with an interest in conservation and in Muir to form The Canadian Friends of John Muir, 'a group of local people with an interest in the conservation of wild places and of the conservation, preservation ethic that John Muir espoused'. In June 1998 and 1999 the Canadian Friends arranged conservation celebrations and public walks through Trout Hollow.

The group spent some time discussing the type of activity they should hold to celebrate the publication of the five letters and the Muir association with Trout Hollow. They decided against any form of academic debate. John Muir wasn't a classroom person; he was a hands-on man – or, more correctly, a feet-on man – and they felt that any event associated with him should be in the same vein. He persuaded people to get out and involve themselves with wild areas – the Canadian Friends decided to do likewise, to offer an event which involved participants in experiencing, in *walking* on the trail of John Muir, rather than hearing or reading about it.

They were also careful to describe the act of putting one foot in front of the other as walking rather than 'hiking', a term which Muir himself detested. Along the walk, the group positioned various experts – a geologist, a local historian, an archaeologist, a 'fern-man' – to set the scene for the walkers.

The probable site of the Trout mill was confirmed by an archaeological dig and the discovery of artifacts from the 1860s. The site for the cabin was suggested by Connie Bresnahan, an Alberta postgraduate student. She noticed in one of Muir's letters that he mentioned watching the mill burn from across the millpond. Walking the wooded area, Connie Bresnahan and Robert Burcher, a Canadian Friend and avocational archaeologist, were able to locate the probable site by eye. Pottery chards spotted in the entrance to a gopher hole and a patch of mortar provided further evidence.

This, of course, is not the end of the story – more of a beginning. Having discovered the site and established its historical importance, what action should now be taken? In some ways, those connected with the site – the Canadian Friends, and the owners, Stanley Knight Limited – are in the same position as John Muir and the Sierra Club, trying many years earlier to take a decision on whether to allow cars into Yosemite Valley. Once you have found a place which has great worth – historic, botanic, scientific, scenic, whatever – and is often beautiful in its own right, what do you do about it? Do you publicise it, encourage everyone to visit it, allow vehicles into or near it? What about the damage that all those feet and wheels will do to the very thing you are trying to protect and preserve? In his later years Muir voted to permit vehicles into Yosemite Valley, wanting as many people as possible to appreciate the beauty with which he had fallen in love. Trout Hollow is obviously a tiny area when compared with the grandeur of Yosemite Valley, but the same principles apply, large or small.

Should the Hollow on the Big Head River be left to its own devices, to stay wild the way it is now – little publicity, few visitors apart from the annual public walk? Is there a compromise solution, with perhaps an interpretative centre in town and a self-guided trail along the riverside? Should the site be developed, given the full Disneyland treatment with an on-site centre, walkways, plaques and Trout Hollow souvenirs? What about recognising it as an invaluable experience for students, and establishing a programme of educational visits, in the spirit of John Muir's life-long crusade to encourage others to interface with the natural world, to get out there? And if funds become available, on what should they be spent? A recent bequest of $25,000 from a local benefactor has provided the Canadian Friends of John Muir with continuing debate on the most appropriate use of the money.

The site lies within the St Vincent township, adjacent to Meaford, and is privately owned by a local company, Stanley Knight Limited, who are very supportive of the work of the Canadian Friends and have no immediate plans to develop the Hollow. They contribute to the annual John Muir walk and allow visits to the site. If you want to see conservation in action, with all its dilemmas and decisions, here it is, just as in John Muir's day. Take a look at it.

CHAPTER 4

To the Gulf and beyond

MUIR WAS TWENTY EIGHT when he left Trout Hollow in 1866, unsure what or where he wanted to be. Instead of going back to Wisconsin he chose Indianapolis, reasoning that the burgeoning industries of the city would provide plentiful job opportunities. He had no difficulty in finding engineering work with a manufacturer of carriage parts, Osgood, Smith and Company. He taught Sunday school occasionally and botanised frequently.

His employers recognised his inventive abilities and he did well with the company. He also established a firm friendship with the Merrill Moores family, friends of his old professor Dr Butler, but he was restless and lonely in the railroad city, debating whether to stay or go.

On 6 March 1867, working late at the factory, he was using a file to adjust a new machine belt. The file slipped and pierced the cornea of his right eye.

> After the first shock was over I closed my eye, and when I lifted the lid of the injured one the aqueous humour dripped on my hand – the sight gradually failed and in a few minutes came perfect darkness. 'My right eye is gone,' I murmured, 'closed forever on all God's beauty.'

With the shock, the sight in his left eye also failed shortly afterwards, and he lay in his bed in darkness, fearing he was blinded for life. His friends send occulists to examine him, and although the doctors prescribed 'a dark room for some weeks', the prognosis was good. The left eye would recover completely and the right, though not perfect, would regain most of its sight.

Lying in that darkened room, dictating letters to his friends, Muir had time to think carefully about his future and what he really wanted to do with it. Jeanne Carr wrote urging him to follow his heart, to listen to his 'good demon', Osgood and Smith offered advancement when he was well again, and in time a partnership in the firm. During those dark weeks Muir came to a life-changing decision; he would leave the city and all its trappings and walk away into the wilderness. His sight might eventually fail, perhaps he would die young, but in the meantime he would spend every available minute in enjoying the wonders of the natural world. There was no time to lose and he 'bade adieu to all my mechanical inventions determined to devote the rest of my life to the study of the inventions of God'.

As soon as he was well enough to travel, and accompanied by young Merrill Moores, he went home to Wisconsin to convalesce for the summer. At the end of August 1867, as he left Hickory Hill, his father asked him to pay for his board and lodging. John did so but vowed that it would be a long time before he visited his father again.

On 1 September, having returned Merrill Moores to his family in Indianapolis, he travelled by train to Louisville, Kentucky.

I steered through the big city by compass without speaking a word to any one. Beyond the city, I found a road running southward, and after passing a scatterment of suburban cabins and cottages I reached the green woods and spread out my pocket map to rough-hew a plan for my journey.

The world, we are told, was made especially for man – a presumption not supported by all the facts.

A Thousand Mile Walk to the Gulf, 1916

He intended to walk southwards by untrodden ways through Kentucky, Tennessee, Georgia, and Florida, to the Gulf of Mexico, from where he hoped to take passage for South America, a place he had long dreamed of visiting. He carried with him a small rubber bag containing only a few toiletries and his three special books, Milton's *Paradise Lost*, a copy of the New Testament and Burns' *Poems*. He took with him only thirty dollars, having been repeatedly warned of the dangers from thieves, intending to sleep rough and eat when he could.

The area through which he walked was

the war-torn country of the Deep South, terribly damaged physically and emotionally by four years of war, by defeat, and by the death of many of its young men. Once prosperous farms and mansions lay neglected or abandoned, bands of desperate men lurked in the woods, preying on travellers, and hungry freed slaves roamed the countryside. Muir had been warned by many friends that he was crazy to attempt such a journey – one thousand miles on foot to the Gulf through a dangerous land. As ever, he paid little attention to such warnings, so great was his need to explore wild areas, so small his concern for personal safety.

Throughout the journey he kept a journal, on the flyleaf of which he wrote 'John Muir, Earth-Planet, Universe', as if in recognition of one man's insignificant stature in the cosmos, but also in recognition of the way in which all living things are interconnected – 'When we try to pick out anything by itself, we find it hitched to everything else in the Universe'. During the walk, his journal shows that this thought was frequently uppermost in his mind, together with despair and disgust at the way in which humans consider themselves separate from the natural world, infinitely superior to plants and animals, which are viewed as provided for our convenience.

The story of the journey, *A Thousand Mile Walk to the Gulf*, was compiled by Frederic William Badè after Muir's death. Based on Muir's 1867 journal, Badè published the book to bridge the chronological gap between Muir's early reminiscences in *The Story of My Boyhood and Youth* and the Californian *My First Summer in the Sierra*. Because it's the first work of any length which we have from Muir, it's particularly interesting in giving us an on-the-spot first person account of his thinking as a young man in his twenties, written as he walked and as his experiences of the war-ravaged South, its flora and fauna, were uppermost in his mind. It's unlikely he intended these thoughts for publication – he made no attempt to publish the account during his lifetime. Many of his comments are refreshingly frank, impassioned, and uncompromisingly against the orthodox thinking of the time on religion, on death, and on the relationship between man and nature.

The only exception to this is the final six paragraphs of

Chapter 8, from 'I followed the Diablo foothills along the San Jose Valley', and Chapter 9, 'Twenty Hill Hollow'. Neither of these sections come from the original journal; they were added by Badè at the time of publication. The first section was contained in a letter to Jeanne Carr, the second originally published as an article in the July 1872 issue of *Overland Monthly*, and the more formal tone sets them solidly apart from the enthusiasm and lyricism of Muir's original.

Many biographers feel it was during the Gulf walk that Muir really came into his own, crystalising the attitudes which were to stay with him for the remainder of his life. It's certainly the first time that we see them expressed in such a coherent form, although it's also perfectly possible that he felt the same way during his first wilderness explorations in Canada – and that we just don't have a journal to confirm it.

It is in *Thousand Mile Walk* that he expresses fully his thoughts on the subject of anthropocentrism, a long word for a simple belief that human beings are the centre of the universe, the only *really* important living things, and that everything else is grist to their mill. Muir abhored this belief and made no bones about it.

> The world, we are told, was made especially for man – a presumption not supported by all the facts. A numerous class of men are painfully astonished whenever they find anything, living or dead, in all God's universe, which they cannot eat or render in some way what they call useful to themselves.
>
> It never seems to occur to these far-seeing teachers that Nature's object in making animals and plants might possibly be first of all the happiness of each one of them, not the creation of all for the happiness of one. Why should man value himself as more than a small part of the one great unit of creation? And what creature of all that the Lord has taken pains to make is not essential to the completeness of that unit – the cosmos? The universe would be incomplete without the smallest transmicroscopic creature that dwells beyond our conceitful eyes and knowledge.

He felt that, for all we know in our complacency, plants and minerals and the land may have senses, feel pain.

Plants are credited with but dim and uncertain sensation, and minerals with positively none at all. But why may not even a mineral arrangement of matter be endowed with sensation of a kind that we in our blind exclusive perfection can have no manner of communication with?

This concept is present in a number of so-called 'primitive' cultures, but in many ways it's remarkable to find it in John Muir, a product of a rigidly structured society and narrow Christian upbringing in the mid nineteenth century. That he was confiding the thought to his diary at this stage demonstrates how far he had already moved from his roots.

Muir also had no time for the image of God painted by 'a numerous class of men'.

He [God] is regarded as a civilised, law-abiding gentleman in favour either of a republic form of government or of a limited monarchy; believes in the literature and language of England, is a warm supporter of the English constitution and Sunday schools and missionary societies, and is purely a manufactured article as any puppet of a half-penny theatre.

Frederick Turner, in his thoughtful study of Muir – *Rediscovering America: John Muir in His Time and Ours* – suggests that as Muir walks towards the Gulf he passes through a threshold between the Calvinistic teachings of his youth and the unorthodoxy of his mature years. There is much to be said in support of this view, particularly on his attitude towards death.

On no subject are our ideas more warped and pitiable than on death.

A Thousand Mile Walk to the Gulf, 1916

On no subject are our ideas more warped and pitiable than on death. Instead of sympathy, the friendly union of life and death so apparent in Nature, we are taught that death is an accident, a deplorable punishment for the oldest sin, the arch-enemy of life, etc. Town children, especially, are steeped in this death orthodoxy, for the natural beauties of death are seldom seen or taught in towns.

Muir did not, of course, spend the entire journey musing on the follies of his fellow man. He tramped through Kentucky, Tennessee, Georgia and Florida, wading through swamps, swimming rivers, losing his way in the forests, and having some narrow escapes. Wild hogs trampled his camp, a band of brigands dismissed him as a 'poor herb doctor' not worth robbing, a horseman stole his bag but returned it after finding nothing worth stealing. In Florida, 'a large, muscular, brawny young negro' who attempted to rob him was discouraged by Muir's firm 'I allow people to find out if I am armed or not'.

Carefully avoiding most of the region's towns, he was astonished at the wildness of mountain areas such as Tennessee. 'On Sundays you may see wild, unshorn, uncombed men coming out of the woods, each with a bag of corn on his back.' 'This is the most primitive country I have seen, primitive in everything. The remotest hidden parts of Wisconsin are far in advance of the mountain regions of Tennessee and North Carolina.'

His innate sense of humour and the ridiculous never seemed to desert him – or if it did, he made no mention of it, belittling the hardships of sleeping on the ground or in farmers' barns and garrets, often going without food for a day or more.

> Travelled today more than forty miles without dinner or supper. No family would receive me, so I had to push on to Augusta. Went hungry to bed and awoke with a sore stomach – sore, I suppose, from its walls rubbing on each other without anything to grind.

His one comment on the swarming snake population was 'Rattlesnakes abundant', and when carried away by a fast-flowing river he 'luckily caught hold of a rock, and after a rest swam and waded ashore. Dragging myself up the steep bank by the overhanging vines, I spread out myself, my paper money, and my plants to dry'.

Accustomed from childhood to hard physical labour and a meagre diet, the thousand miles probably didn't seem particularly rigorous to Muir. He was doing what he wanted to, botanising, tramping, staying away from the bump and grind of the cities. There is in his journal a repetition of the word 'escape' – 'Escaped from the dust and squalor of my garret bedroom to the glorious forest', 'I escaped to the fields', 'Escaped from a heap of uncordial kindness to the generous bosom of the woods'.

The careful attention which he gave to plants was also directed at humans, often in a humourous way.

> Travelled in the wake of three poor but merry mountaineers – an old woman, a young woman, and a young man – who sat, leaned, and lay in the box of a shackly wagon that seemed to be held together by spiritualism, and was kept in agitation by a very large and a very small mule. In going down hill the looseness of the harness and the joints of the wagon allowed the mules to back nearly out of sight beneath the box, and the three who occupied it were slid against the front boards in a heap over the mules' ears. Before they could unravel their limbs from this unmannerly and impolite disorder, a new ridge in the road frequently tilted them with a swish and a bump against the back boards in a mixing that was still more grotesque.

> I expected to see man, women, and mules mingled in piebald ruin at the bottom of some rocky hollow, but they seemed to have full confidence in the back board and front board of the wagon-box. So they continued to slide comfortably up and down, from end to end, in slippery obedience to the law of gravitation, as the grades demanded. Where the jolting was moderate, they engaged in conversation on love, marriage, and camp-meetings, according to the custom of the country. The old lady, through all the vicissitudes of the transportation, held a bouquet of French marigolds.

Muir's route took him across the Ohio River and into Kentucky, over the Cumberland Mountains of Tennessee – 'the first mountain scenery I ever beheld' – and down to the coastal city of Savannah, Georgia, where he had arranged for money to await him at the post office. The money had not arrived and his pockets were empty. Worried about sleeping on the streets of Savannah – '... idle negroes were prowling about everywhere, and I was afraid' – he came to the Bonaventure graveyard, just outside the town. 'Bonaventure is called a graveyard, a town of the dead, but the few graves are powerless in such a depth of life.' Spanish moss draped itself graciously from the live-oak trees, flocks of birds – warblers, crows, bald eagles – and gaudy butterflies made the graveyard their home. Muir was enchanted, and for the several days that his money took to arrive, he spent each night in the graveyard, nestling like a bird in a 'thicket of sparkleberry bushes'. Again in his account he makes light of the discomfort, mentioning only 'a lot of hungry stinging mosquitoes' and a 'cold-blooded creature' who attempted to share his bed.

> ... whether a snake or simply a frog or toad I do not know, but instinctively, instead of drawing back my hand, I grasped the poor creature and threw it over the tops of the bushes. That was the only significant disturbance or fright that I got.

Bonaventure graveyard is still a beautiful place and you can visit it today. By car it's approximately fifteen minutes from the centre of Savannah. Take Victory Drive and turn left on Bonaventure Road. The graveyard has achieved fame in recent years for a reason which has absolutely nothing to do with John Muir. It features in John Berendt's bestselling *Midnight in the Garden of Good and Evil*, which was also made into a film. The resultant publicity means that anyone in Savannah who hasn't been away on Mars can tell you where the graveyard is, and tourist organisations run regular tours to the cemetery. Don't expect, though, to see the now famous statue of the girl with two bowls, which appears on *Midnight*'s cover. The family who owned the statue became so unamused with visitors traipsing over their family plot that they passed the stone figure on to the Telfair Museum at 121 Barnard Street, Savannah.

Savannah itself is rightly famed for its beautiful houses and squares and trees, and you can happily spend days there, exploring its beauties. That is not what Muir did, though, as towns were not his favourite places; on his walk to the Gulf, he avoided them wherever possible and only gave favourable mentions to Athens, in Georgia, and Gainesville, Florida.

By the time his money arrived several days later he was faint with hunger. He bought a generous helping of gingerbread, 'had a large regular meal on top', and hot-footed it out of town. By mid October he had reached Florida, crossing from Savannah to

Fernandina on the steamer *Sylvan Shore*. There he followed the railroad to the Florida Keys, botanising as he travelled and astonished at the vegetation. '... in Florida came the greatest change of all, for here grows the palmetto, and here blow the winds so strangely toned by them. These palms and these winds severed the last strands of the cord that united me with home.'

In Florida, too, he felt very alone in an alien land. 'The winds are full of strange sounds, making one feel far from the people and plants and fruitful fields of home. Night is coming on and I am filled with indescribable loneliness.' Walking towards the coast, he 'caught the scent of the salt breeze' and was at once transported to Dunbar,

> its rocky coast, winds and waves... Forgotten were the palms and magnolias and the thousand flowers that enclosed me. I could see only dulse and tangle, long-winged gulls, the Bass Rock in the Firth of Forth, and the old castle, schools, churches, and long country rambles in search of birds' nests.

At Cedar Keys, discovering he would have to wait a couple of weeks before the next steamer, Muir took work at Hodgson's sawmill. On the third day, returning to the mill, he fell and lay unconscious on the path. Dragging himself painfully back to the mill lodging house, he begged the watchman to help him to his bed, but the man, thinking him to be drunk, refused. On his hands and knees, Muir eventually reached his bed and remembered nothing more until he woke in the Hodgsons' house some days later. It was malaria. For three months the Hodgsons nursed him, administering quinine and chamomile, and he never forgot how they took him into their home and saved his life.

The Hodgsons' house, subsequently demolished, stood on a hill two miles north of town, and from it Muir sketched Lime Key while he was convalescing. By January 1868 he felt able to go on his way, although still frail and subject to occasional bouts of fever. The schooner *Island Belle* was bound for Cuba and for twenty five dollars he took passage on her, enjoying a magnificent storm just as he had on his first sea voyage from Glasgow to New York.

He spent the following month in Havana, sleeping on the schooner, botanising by day in the flower-filled pastures and on Morro Hill, and regretting that he was still not strong enough to explore the mountainous centre of Cuba. Alexander von Humboldt, who wrote extensively on his own South American travels and whose forest conservation beliefs greatly influenced Muir, had spoken of 'the unseen and unwalked' ranges, but for the moment Muir had to be content with his botany studies. He liked the Cubans he encountered but was appalled at their attitude towards animals. 'I saw more downright brutal cruelty to mules and horses during the few weeks I stayed there than in my whole life elsewhere.'

> *Death is a kind nurse saying 'Come children, to bed and get up in the morning' – a gracious Mother calling her children home.*
>
> Undated journal entry

Unable to find a vessel bound for South America, he decided to travel north to California by way of New York, hoping that the crisp air of the Californian mountains would restore his health. He wasn't abandoning the trip to South America, just postponing it for a year, he told himself. It was to be a great deal longer before he finally reached the tropics, and by the time he did so he would be a nationally known figure.

Taking passage on a boat filled to the deck rails with oranges – a third of which were rotten by the time the boat docked – Muir sailed from the tropical heat of Cuba to the ice floes of New York. 'For myself, long burdened with fever, the frosty wind, as it sifted through my loosened bones, was more delicious and grateful than ever was a spring-scented breeze.'

In New York he stayed close to the harbour, worried about losing his way in the maze of streets and rushing people. 'Often I thought I would like to explore the city if, like a lot of wild hills and valleys, it was clear of inhabitants.' Able to find his way through trackless swamps and forests in the wilderness, he was uncertain, uncomfortable in the city, a characteristic which never left him. Years later, meeting his editor, Robert Underwood Johnson, at San Francisco's Palace Hotel, he lost his bearings somewhere between the hotel foyer and Johnson's room. Johnson recalls hearing Muir's voice echoing down the corridors, 'Johnson, Johnson! Where are you? I can't get the hang of these artificial canyons'.

On 6 March 1868 Muir embarked on the next stage of his voyage to California, sailing on the *Santiago de Cuba* for Aspinwall-Colon, on the Isthmus of Panama, and remarking adversely on his four hundred fellow passengers, 'Never had I seen such a barbarous mob, especially at meals'. (One wonders what they did at meals – food fights, perhaps, or all-you-can-eat contests?) He concluded that the only truly unclean animal was man, was enthralled with the Isthmus crossing and its 'glorious fauna', and promised himself that this was another place to which he must return.

From the western shores of the Isthmus, the *Nebraska* took him up the coast to San Francisco. Arriving there in late March 1868, he lost no time in leaving town. The story goes that he stopped a man in the street and asked for 'the nearest way out of town to the wild part of the State'. With him was a young Englishman, a cockney named Joseph Chillwell, whom he had met on the Nebraska and who also wanted to see the mountains of California.

CHAPTER 5

California and 'The Range of Light'

WALKING EASTWARDS OUT OF San Francisco towards the mountains, Muir and Chilwell reached the Pacheco Pass, overlooking 'the floweriest part of the world I had yet seen'. Over a hundred miles ahead of them lay the Sierra Nevada, the mountains with which John Muir would develop a lifelong love affair and which he named 'the Range of Light'. This was his first sight of their beauty, his first taste of the exhilarating affect of breathing mountain air, and for the rest of his life he sought to repeat the experience. 'We were new creatures, born again; and truly not until this time were we fairly conscious that we were born at all.'

But the walk also had its dangers – and its humour.

The two men stopped briefly for provisions at Coulterville in the Mariposa foothills, where the storekeeper persuaded them to buy 'an old army musket' in case they encountered bears in the mountains. Desperate for some meat to augment their 'flour and water' diet, Chilwell, a poor shot, persuaded Muir to test the gun and give him shooting lessons. Sighting a mark on a shanty wall and warning Chilwell to stay clear, Muir fired.

> I supposed that he [Chilwell] had gone some distance back of the cabin, but instead he went inside of it and stood up against the mark that he had himself placed on the wall, and as the shake wall of soft sugar pine was only about half an inch thick, the shot passed through it and into his shoulder. He came rushing out with his hand on his shoulder, crying in great concern, 'You've shot me, you've shot me, Scottie'.

Luckily for Chilwell the weather was cold and he was wearing a total of three overcoats and three shirts. Burrowing beneath these layers, Muir had no difficulty in extracting the shot with the tip of his penknife, but his opinion of Englishmen was not improved by the incident. For the remainder of their trip, Chilwell continued in his efforts to acquire fresh meat, encouraging his companion to take pot shots at a brown bear, quail, grouse, numerous jackrabbits and a burrowing owl. As Muir 'took good care to warn the poor beasts by making myself and the gun conspicuous', Chilwell's diet remained largely meat free despite his hopeful attempts.

It is apparent from Muir's account that the two men enjoyed their trip together, teasing each other over their national characteristics and differences. Muir liked to sleep outside, Chilwell 'had the house habit'; Muir was eager to meet the mountain animals, Chilwell wary, particularly of bears – 'the abundance of bear tracks caused Mr Chilwell no little alarm'; Muir was happy to subsist on a meagre diet, Chilwell hankered for flesh and never tired of telling people of 'the meanness and misery of so pure a vegetable diet as was ours on the Yosemite trip. 'Just think of it', said he, 'we lived a whole month on flour and water!'

These differences did not impede their friendship. Muir, like most of us, had a great liking for human company, particularly company which could appreciate the wilderness. He has sometimes been depicted as a man who sought isolation, separation from his fellows and his family, yet his reminiscences and accounts written by his friends say something very different. On his first excursion into the Sierra he was happy to be accompanied by Chilwell; during his early days in Yosemite he took with him a young friend, Harry Randall, who shared his Yosemite creek cabin; and on his solitary journey to the Gulf of Mexico he many times noted in his journal how alone he felt, how he longed for companionship.

One day's exposure to mountains is better than cartloads of books.

Undated journal entry

After working on the harvest at Hopeton in the autumn of 1868, Chilwell went on his way. Muir stayed on, doing a variety of jobs – breaking mustangs, ferry boating, sheep shearing, and spending the winter shepherding for a local character by the name of Smoky Jack. Inheriting the previous shepherd's 'dismal little hut', he remained with his flock until the spring, closely observing the behaviour of the ground squirrels and the jackrabbits, the meadow larks, plovers and eagles, and falling ever deeper in love with the landscape.

In the spring, casting around for a way to return to the Sierra without starving, he accepted an offer from Pat Delaney, a neighbour of Smoky Jack's. Delaney, whom Muir nicknamed Don Quixote, suggested he accompany the flock to their summer pasture in the high Sierra. In return for keeping an eye on Delaney's shepherd, Muir would be free to botanise as much as he wanted. Muir delightedly accepted the offer, and from this experience came *My First Summer in the Sierra*, published over forty years later and based on the notebooks kept during those sheep herding months of 1869.

Despite the fact that the final version was put together many years later, the writing retains much of the freshness and enthusiasm which Muir experienced at the time. It remains for many readers their 'favourite' Muir, its prose ecstatic, lyrical, and sometimes downright over-the-top. He finds it increasingly difficult to pen a paragraph without mentioning the objects of his devotion. 'Lovemonument mountains', he calls the high Sierra; cumuli he terms 'mountains of the sky', fondly tending the flora beneath them; 'we are now in the mountains and they are in us, kindling enthusiasm, making every nerve quiver, filling every pore and cell of us'.

It is difficult to stand aloof, though, to be critical, such is his adoration, his whole-hearted, whole-bodied love.

> Oh, these vast, calm, measureless mountain days, inciting at once to work and rest! Days in whose light everything seems equally divine, opening a thousand windows to show us God. Nevermore, however weary, should one faint by the way who gains the blessings of one mountain day; whatever his fate, long life, short life, stormy or calm, he is rich forever.

Muir's enthusiasm often led him into dangerous situations, as when he climbed down into Yosemite Falls to get a closer look at the stupendous fall of water. '... the slope beside it looked dangerously smooth and steep, and the swift roaring flood beneath, overhead, and beside me was very nerve trying. I there-

John Muir circa 1870
by kind permission of John Muir National Historic Site

John Muir circa 1900
by kind permission of John Muir National Historic Site

Indianapolis, January 6th, 1867

My true friend Harriet,

So long and good a letter as your last should have been answered long ago, but you know my tardy habits in correspondence matters and will not, I'm pretty sure, interpret my long silence to my disadvantage.

What you say upon friendship is all true, and I believe & feel it all, I confess Hattie, that the deep substantial warmth of your feelings a little surprises me and I never thought to find in you so true a friend – Hattie. I suppose because I was sure I did not deserve such, I was peavish and irritable when living in the hollow and said some cruel words that have often pained me since and do so more and more when I see that you are so warmhearted and good. I am sure that if I were to live another year in the hollow I would not say a single unkind word to any of you however much I might be fretted. Before your troubles came we did not know each other but when the blow of adversity fell upon the (*fill*) of your hearts it proved its metal.

I am much obliged to you for so minute an account of that matter twixt Charlie & Missus. The next time they marry Chas considerately promises to send me an invitation. I rec'd his letter a day or two before yours, but of course a (*savie*) of descriptions would not be sufficient for so remarkable an event.

I wonder where you all are now, – is it so that after your sore partings and sail on the wide cold outside sea you have gathered, and again nestle in quiet in your tranquil hollow. If so I am sure that you will enjoy each other's society more, if possible, than ever. The peacefulness of your hollow will be still more peaceful, and all the comforts of home will glow with a keener charm, and who will say that blessings so great are not worth even all the price you have paid. I am gratified to hear of your father's health, and sorry that Maggie is so unwell.

You ask what church I attend – generally that of the disciples, and I teach a class in a Mission Sunday school. I feel as though I should do more in this direction.

Danie is still in Mich. I think he is engaged in some speculations. He sent me a new fern. I found six new ferns this summer. I have the gift of some english ferns in prospect There is a moss which closely infests the trunks of trees in wet places. I have gathered hundreds of handfuls in Canada in the vain hope of finding a fruited specimen, judge of my delight in finding it fruited here, and the same is the case with other species. I was made happy a few days ago by a visit from prof. Butler. He kindly sought me out and I enjoyed his conversations a whole evening at the house of one of his friends. Mrs. Carr lent me her copy of that book she spoke of in Canada. Her letters are interesting as ever and are becoming more confidingly friendly. I am in still another home, the fifth since last spring. I have a room with a (restters) bedstand and I have framed my pictures. I spent about a day in retouching the hollow and it looks natural in its nice frame.

Johnny Boise still looks manlike across the pond just at the flume.

Tell Rachel that I hope she will always have plenty of sunshine to fill her large happy eyes. That David Galloway will always remember her – without marking it down.

I have been so exceeding busy that my face is still unphotographed.

I will write to the boys soon.

Remember me to all who care to hear from me.

Take my warmest greetings & wishes for happiness in sixty seven

John Muir's letter to Harriet Trout, dated 6 January 1867. This letter is one of the five Muir letters recently made public in Meaford, Ontario.
Reproduced in full overleaf by kind permission of the Meaford Museum

Indpl's Jan 6th 67

My true friend Harriet —
So long and good a letter as your
last should have been answered
long ago, but you know my tardy
habits in correspondence matters,
and will not, I'm pretty sure,
interpret my long silence to my
disadvantage —
What you say upon friendship
is all true, and I believe & feel it
all, I confess Hatt that the
deep substantial warmth of your
feelings a little surprises me,
and I never thought to find
in you so true a friend — partly
I suppose because I was sure I did
not deserve such, I was peevish
and irritable when living in the
Hollow and said some cruel
words that have often pained
me since and do so more & more

Take my warmest greetings & wishes for Happy

Remember me to all who care to hear from me

nets in sixty seven. I will write to the boys
when I see that you are so
so warmhearted and good,
I am sure that if I were to
live another year in the Wallou
I would not say a single unkind
word to any of you however much
I might be fretted. Before your
troubles came we did not know
each other but when the blow
of adversity — fell upon the steel
of your hearts — it proved its metal.

I am much obliged to you
for so minute an account of
that matter twixt Charlie & Mideno
The next time they marry, Chas
considerately promises to send
me an invitation, I recd his
letter a day or two before yours,
but of course a score of descriptions would not be sufficient
for so markable an event —
I wonder where you all are
now, — is it so that after your

unphotographed

I have been so exercising busy that my time is still

love partings and sail on the
wide cold outside sea You have
gathered, and again nestle in
quiet in your tranquil hollow,
if so I am sure that you will
enjoy each others society more if
possible than ever. The peacefulness
of your hollow will be still more
peaceful, and all the comforts
of home will glow with a keener
charm. And who will say that
blessings so great are not worth
even all the price you have paid,
I am gratified to hear of your
fathers health, and sorry that
Maggie is so unwell -
You ask What church I attend
Generally that of. The disciples.
And I teach a class in a Mission
Sunday school, I feel as though I should
do more in this direction —
Danie is still in Mich, I think he
is engaged in some speculation

Tell Rachel that I hope she
will always have plenty of sunshine
to fill her large happy eyes

He sent me a new fern, I found
six new ferns this summer I have
the gift of some english ferns in
prospect. There is a moss which closely
invests the trunks of trees in wet places
I have gathered hundreds of handfuls
in Canada in the vain hope of finding
a fruited specimen, judge of my delight
in finding it fruited here, and the
same is the case with other species
I was made happy a few days ago by a
visit from Prof Butler, he kindly sought
me out and I enjoyed his conversation
a whole evening at the house of
one of his friends, Mrs Carr lent
me her copy of that book she spoke
of in Canada, her letters are interesting as ever and are becoming more
confidingly friendly, I am in still
another house the fifth since last spring
I have a room with a rattless bedstead
and I have framed my pictures
I spent about a day in retouching the
hollow and it looks natural in its nice
frame

John Muir on the Merced River at the Royal Arches in Yosemite Valley
by kind permission of Charles and Nina Bradley

fore concluded not to venture farther, but did nevertheless.' He comes to no harm, although the memory of it keeps him awake most of the night.

He also – at least in retrospect – retains his sense of humour when confronted by danger, in one instance in the person of a bear.

> ... I thought I should like to see his gait in running, so I made a sudden rush at him, shouting and swinging my hat to frighten him, expecting to see him make haste to get away. But to my dismay he did not run or show any sign of running. On the contrary, he stood his ground ready to fight and defend himself, lowered his head, thrust it forward, and looked sharply and fiercely at me. Then I suddenly began to fear that upon me would fall the work of running ...

He comes to despise the flock – 'hoofed locusts' he terms them – eating all before them, trampling the wild flowers of the glacial meadows. Nor does he think much better of the sheep owners, concerned only with their profits, or of the Californian shepherd, 'never quite sane for any considerable time'. His description of Billy the shepherd and his trousers is a classic study, rich in irony and powers of observation.

> Following the sheep he carries a heavy six-shooter swung from his belt on one side and his luncheon on the other. The ancient cloth in which the meat, fresh from the frying pan, is tied serves as a filter through which the clear fat and gravy juices drip down on his right hip and leg in clustering stalactites. This oleaginous formation is soon broken up however, and diffused and rubbed evenly into his scanty apparel, by sitting down, rolling over, crossing his legs while resting on logs, making shirt and trousers watertight and shiny. His trousers, in particular, have become so adhesive with the mixed fat and resin that pine needles, thin flakes and fibres of bark hair, mica scales and minute grains of quartz, hornblende, etc, feathers, seed wings, moth and butterfly wings, legs and antennae of innumerable insects, or even whole insects such as the small beetles, moths and mosquitoes, with flower petals, pollen dust and indeed bits of all plants, animals and minerals of the region adhere to them and are safely embedded, so that though far from being a naturalist he collects fragmentary specimens of everything and becomes

richer than he knows. His specimens are kept passably fresh too, by the purity of the air and the resiny bituminous beds into which they are pressed. Man is a microcosm, at least our shepherd is, or rather his trousers. These precious overalls are never taken off, and nobody knows how old they are, though one may guess by their thickness and concentric structure. Instead of wearing thin they wear thick, and in their stratification have no small geological significance.

Muir forms unfavourable opinions on the region's Indians – 'the worst thing about them is their uncleanliness' – and finds he has an even greater dislike for the 'glaring tailored tourists' who are beginning to find their way into the Yosemite. He establishes a close relationship with his companion Carlo, 'a wondrous wise dog', and reiterates in *My First Summer in the Sierra* his belief in the 'connectedness' of all living things, man, dog, plant – 'when we try to pick out anything by itself, we find it hitched to everything else in the universe ...'.

It's at this stage in his life that Muir, for the first time, feels an inner sense trying to tell him something. This feeling would come to him twice more in his life, warning him of the deaths of his parents. He didn't understand it, made light of it, but accepted it. In this case, he had a premonition that his old Wisconsin professor, James Butler, was down below him in Yosemite Valley. Hurriedly changing into the only clean clothes he had, Muir did indeed discover Butler above Vernal Fall. The two friends spent the evening together, delighting in each other's company, but Muir was relieved to escape the following morning to his beloved mountains, pitying the poor professor, 'compelled to dwell with lowland care and dust and din'.

It is also during his first summer in the Sierra that Muir becomes convinced that, contrary to popular belief at the time, the area's landscape was created by glacial action. Climbing Mount Dana, exploring Lake Tenaya and Tuolumne Meadows, he notes that 'almost every yard ... shows the scoring and polishing action of a great glacier ...'. Josiah D. Whitney, head of the California Geological Survey and author of the 1869 *Yosemite Guide-Book*, was the acknowledged expert in the field, and believed that

Yosemite and the Sierra had been formed aeons ago by violent upheaval – the subsidence or catastrophe theory, as it is known. Muir, influenced by the theories of Louis Agassiz and by Ezra Carr's lectures at Madison, felt that Whitney was mistaken. Subsequent study would prove Muir to be correct.

But, for the moment, he was more enthralled by the sheer beauty of these mountains and his need to return to them. At the end of that first summer, accompanying the flock back to the lowlands, he wrote 'I have crossed the Range of Light, surely the brightest and best of all the Lord has built, and rejoicing in its glory, I gladly, gratefully, hopefully pray I may see it again'.

It would be only a short while before his hopes were realised. In mid November of that year, unable to stay away any longer, Muir returned to Yosemite in the company of a young Philadelphian, Harry Randall, who had also been working for Pat Delaney. Muir secured jobs for both of them at James Hutchings' Upper Hotel in Yosemite Valley and wrote to Jeanne Carr 'I am dead and gone to heaven'.

Helped by Randall, he built a sawmill for Hutchings, utilising fallen pine trees to renovate the hotel and to build modesty partitions between the guests' beds. Tourists were beginning to find their way into the Valley in larger numbers and many of them were affronted to discover that the bedroom partitions at Hutchings' hotel were made only of thin fabric. Later, when Muir's name was known throughout the US as a conservationist and protector of forests, his detractors accused him (and Hutchings) of cutting live trees for the sawmill. Muir always vehemently denied this, stating that only 'downed wood' had been used.

He built a cabin on Yosemite Creek, below the great Fall, and today the cabin site is marked by a plaque which reads

John Muir built here a sugar pine cabin in 1869 and made it his home for two years. In commemoration of the noble service which this friend and protector of nature rendered to the people of the United States, this tablet has been placed here in 1924 by the California Conference of Social Work.

What the plaque doesn't mention is the number of mosquitoes who also make the creek their home during the spring and early summer – lavish use of insect repellent is strongly recommended unless you have a fancy for spending the next few days scratching like a demented chimpanzee. You can find the plaque and its mosquitoes when you walk down from Yosemite Falls towards the road – just follow the course of Yosemite Creek.

John Muir doesn't mention the mosquitoes either – well, much of the time he spent at the cabin was in the winter (no mosquitoes). He was also, of course, one of those hardy types not given to complaining, and wore far better protection than the shorts and tee-shirts of today. His habitual attire was long trousers, long-sleeved shirt, waistcoat and jacket, with shoes rather than boots because of the greater range of ankle movement shoes gave him. He rarely wore a coat of any kind when walking or climbing, preferring the freedom of movement to the added warmth – coats in his time were invariably heavyweight.

The stream ran through the cabin, and over his desk Muir trained an archway of ferns in which tiny tree frogs 'made fine music in the night'. From his window he had a clear view of Yosemite Falls, and in his all too short spare time he explored, climbed and botanised through the snow-bound winter of 1869 and the following spring. For Yosemite Valley, with its water meadows and towering formations, he developed a deep and protective love which made him scorn the chattering tourists – 'finished and finite clods', he called them – untouched by the Valley's grandeur.

In November 1871 he saw for the first time the beautiful valley of Hetch Hetchy, describing it as the 'Tuolumne Yosemite'. From two miles above Hetch Hetchy, he descended into the canyon by a bear-path, camped out in bear territory 'because I knew that bears never eat men where berries and acorns abound', and wrote glowingly of the valley's special beauty.

Above all, he loved the great towering shape and presence of Yosemite's Half Dome, known to the Indians as Tissiack. 'Never have I beheld so great and so gentle and so divine a piece of ornamental work as this grand gray dome in its first winter mantle woven and jeweled in a night.' Tissiack has not changed. Yosemite Valley is now a tourist mecca, with museums and visitor centres, stores, parking lots and campgrounds, but Tissiack and El Capitan stand as they have for thousands of years, dwarfing the Valley floor and its humans.

What also hasn't changed, for too many tourists, is their reaction to the beauty surrounding them. John Muir despaired of the way in which visitors came to Yosemite, stared but did not see, looked inward and were preoccupied with the lack of home comforts rather than looking outward at the mountains. He wanted as many people as possible to visit Yosemite – later in life, he supported the motion to allow vehicles into the Valley – and to be altered by the experience, to find the physical and spiritual renewal which he had discovered there. So if you're *On the Trail of John Muir*, don't get bogged down in the museums or by the hot-dog stands and souvenirs. By all means stock up with their goodies, but don't leave it at that. Do what John Muir did. Walk in Tuolomne Meadows, the Sierra's largest subalpine meadow, among the wild flowers of early summer, or under Muir's beloved giant sequoia trees in the Mariposa Grove, thirty five miles south of the Valley. Walk or drive to Glacier Point, where from a height of 3,200 feet there's a panoramic view of Yosemite Valley, with Tissiack in the foreground and the snow-covered peaks of the High Sierra in the distance. Try to be there at sunset or under a full moon and you'll understand the spell which bound Muir to the Valley.

Over ninety percent of Yosemite's 760,000 acres is designated as protected wilderness. You can get a permit to camp out in many parts; you can walk one of the many trails. The John Muir Trail runs approximately 220 miles from Happy Isles at the upper end of Yosemite Valley to Mount Whitney/Whitney Portal at its southern end. There are black bears in the woods, and most of the trail lies above 9,000 feet, so unless you're an experienced snow traveller this means you need to walk it in summer. En route you will pass peaks topping 13,000 feet, thousands of icy-cold sparkling lakes and streams, canyons diving down thousands of feet, and no surfaced roads for 140 miles from the northern Tioga Pass to

I am hopelessly and forever a mountaineer.

Letter written from Yosemite Valley to Jeanne Carr, 7 October 1874

Sherman Pass in the south. There are a number of stride-by-stride guides to the trail – you can find details of these in the bibliography – and you'll need a wilderness permit (Wilderness Reservations, PO Box 545, Yosemite, CA 95389).

The trail also traverses the John Muir Wilderness, created in 1965 and expanded in 1984. Its 581,000 acres comprise the largest and most-visited wilderness area in California. For overnight use you need a permit (there's no charge), but obtain your permit well in advance as there's a quota system operating during the summer months and all permits are normally gone by the end of May. The simplest way to reach the wilderness is via US Highway 395, turning west on State Highway 203 and driving nineteen miles to Devil's Postpile National Monument, from where you can head south on the John Muir Trail.

There's a wealth of publications available on Yosemite (again, see the bibliography), and you can obtain free information and maps by writing to Yosemite National Park, CA 95389-0577 USA, or by visiting the website at *www.nps.gov/yose*. There is hotel accommodation and camping available in the Valley, visitor centres in the Valley and at Tuolumne Meadows and Wawona, bus tours to the main attractions, a bus shuttle service and bike hire on the Valley floor, and numerous summer time sporting and interpretive activities. A plan is under way to limit the number of private vehicles in the Valley by bussing tourists in. Parking lots and roads now cover what should be open meadows and wetlands ... Summer weekends can bring more than 7,000 cars to the narrow floor of Yosemite Valley. Would John Muir be appalled or pleased?

Winter snow often closes roads, and the eastern approach on Route 120 via the 9,945 foot Tioga Pass is inaccessible from November to May. From the west, Route 120 connects Manteca to the park, Route 41 brings you from Fresno to the south entrance near the Mariposa Grove, and Route 140 connects Merced, Mariposa, and El Portal with the Arch Rock entrance.

The simplest way to reach Hetch Hetchy is to enter the park via Route 120, turning north on Evergreen Road, shortly before the Big Oak Flat Entrance to the park. Turn right at Camp Mather to follow Hetch Hetchy Road – again, you will need a wilderness permit to camp out in the area.

None of these roads were there in Muir's time. He didn't, anyway, have much time for roads. Occasionally he rode a mustang by the name of Brownie (sometimes Brownie is referred to as a mule, so there was probably more than one Brownie), but mostly he walked, carrying dried bread and tea, no gun, no coat, no camping gear. He generally slept rough, even in the winter, relying on the warmth of a large campfire at night, although occasionally he would find himself caught out by a severe storm. On one such occasion, on a mountain top, knowing that he must stay awake or perish, he spent the night doing the Highland Fling.

While his employer Hutchings was absent in Washington, he befriended the rest of the Hutchings family. The three children, Charlie, Floy and Cosie, became very dear to him, and his continuing affection for them was recalled many years later by the adult Cosie, Mrs Gertrude Hutchings Mills. He also formed a close friendship with Hutchings' wife, Elvira, who shared his love of plants. There was speculation in the Valley at the time as to whether there was more than friendship between them, although given Muir's narrow upbringing, Elvira's devout Christianity, the somewhat rigid morals of the 1870s, and the presence in the household of Elvira's mother, who rejoiced in the name of Florantha Sproat, this seems unlikely.

Muir's relationships with women in Yosemite – or at any other time – are difficult to assess. He enjoyed their company, sought them as friends, but appeared to fight shy of any romantic entanglement. Some biographers have suggested that he knew – subconsciously or otherwise – that what he needed to accomplish in the wilderness was not compatible with such a relationship and that he selected women friends who were in some way unsuitable or unattainable.

One of his closest friendships was with Jeanne Carr, with whom he carried on a regular and affectionate correspondence.

She, of course, was married to Professor Ezra Carr (a difficult man, by all accounts, twice fired from teaching positions) and was therefore unavailable, but a number of commentators have suggested that it was Jeanne Carr who was his true soulmate.

Therese Yelverton, a well-known British writer who arrived in the Valley in the summer of 1870, also took a liking to Muir and made him the hero of her novel *Zanita*, published in 1872. She calls him Kenmuir, and in purple prose elevates him to hero status, with 'open blue eyes of honest questioning, and glorious auburn hair'. Muir lent her his herbariums, shared his glaciation theories with her and acted as her guide in Yosemite. William Frederic Badè describes Therese as a 'warm friend' of Muir and some biographers have suggested that she became infatuated with him, pursuing him until he felt it necessary to leave the Valley for a while. Margaret Salborn, in *Yosemite: Its Discovery, Its Wonders, and Its People*, dismisses this as nonsense, saying Therese was far too level-headed to indulge in infatuation, and gives a riveting account of Therese's adventure-packed life, including a near fatal accident in Yosemite.

With Hutchings away in Washington, and with Jeanne Carr sending many of her friends and acquaintances to seek him out in Yosemite, Muir increasingly found himself acting as the local guide. When Hutchings returned to find that many Yosemite visitors were asking to see his sawyer, he was not amused. The relationship worsened, although Muir continued in his employ until the autumn of 1871.

In August 1870 his visitors included Joseph Le Conte, the eminent geologist from the University of California, who agreed with Muir's theory that Yosemite had been formed by glacial action. So, in September 1871, did another visitor, John D. Runkle, President of the Massachusetts Institute of Technology. Encouraged by their support, by Jeanne Carr's belief in his abilities, and by his own discovery of a living glacier at Red Mountain in the Merced group, Muir felt bold enough to attempt publication of his beliefs. To his surprise the *New York Tribune* accepted the article, entitled 'Yosemite Glaciers', and printed it in their 5 December 1871 issue.

But before that article appeared, Muir had experienced one of the great moments of his life – a meeting with Ralph Waldo

Emerson, America's intellectual giant and philosopher. Muir had built for himself a 'hang-bird's hang-nest' attached to one wall of the sawmill, in which he slept and studied. One day, to his surprise and delight, up the makeshift ladder into the hang-nest climbed the sixty-eight year old Emerson. During the short time that Emerson remained in the Valley, the two men became firm friends and established a high mutual

Climb the mountains and get their good tidings.

Our National Parks, 1901

regard, although Muir was deeply disappointed that Emerson felt himself too old to camp out. Emerson added John Muir's name to his list of great men; Muir paid Emerson the ultimate compliment of likening him to his favourite tree – 'Emerson was the most serene, majestic, sequoia-like soul I ever met'.

With the publication of 'Yosemite Glaciers', Muir was launched on his writing career. He toiled away at it, never finding it easy, hating the time that it took him and longing to be in the mountains. But the public loved it and wanted more. On New Year's Day 1872 the *Tribune* published 'Yosemite in Winter', and in April he started to write for the *Overland Monthly*. 'The Yosemite Valley in Flood' was followed by 'Twenty Hill Hollow', 'Living Glaciers of California', and 'Mountain Building'.

In the winter he wrote, staying with friends in Oakland. It was at this time, too, that he formed a lifelong friendship with the Swetts. John Swett, State Superintendent of Schools for California, and his wife, Mary, welcomed Muir into their San Francisco house, which for five years became his home when in town.

In the good weather he went back up into his beloved mountains. There were expeditions with Emily Pelton, Jeanne Carr, William Keith; to Yosemite, Kings River, Lake Tahoe; and now when Muir returned to Yosemite Valley he found himself a celebrity. His continued his careful examinations of glacial activity, and his skill and experience as a mountaineer grew apace. He climbed Mount Shasta and Mount Ritter, where he came to a trembling standstill on a seemingly impassable ledge but was saved by some incomprehensible force – 'The other self, bygone experiences,

Instinct, or Guardian Angel – call it what you will ...' High on Mount Watkins he had another narrow escape, falling and knocking himself out on the granite. Coming round, he found that a fall of a thousand feet had been blocked only by the small bushes in which he was lying, and forced himself to make the climb again, upbraiding himself for soft living on his city visits – 'There, that is what you get by intercourse with stupid town stairs and dead pavements!'

In a letter to Jeanne Carr he declared '... I care to live only to entice people to look at Nature's loveliness. My own special self is nothing.' His April 1875 'Wild Wool' in the *Overland Monthly* pursues this theme, and in January 1876 he delivered his first public lecture, on glaciers and forests, to the Literary Institute of Sacramento. Shy by nature and horribly nervous, he was put at ease by looking at an alpine landscape of William Keith's, set up in front of him as he spoke. Keith, a Scot born in the same year as Muir, had come to him in Yosemite in 1872, and the two men, despite many differences, remained close friends, teasing each other mercilessly and sharing the same ironic Scots sense of humour. The painting at the lecture had been Keith's idea – 'You can look at that, Johnnie,' he said, 'and imagine you are in the mountains' – and the confidence that it gave Muir enabled him to plead the cause of conservation.

Appalled at the way his beloved trees were being felled by the burgeoning lumber industry, he wrote his first essay on forest conservation, 'God's First Temples: How Shall We Preserve Our Forests?', published in the Sacramento Record-Union of 9 February 1876, and wrote movingly that 'the flowers I used to watch and love are mostly dead'. He pleaded with his readers to realise the immeasurable value of the mountains, not only for their scenic beauty but as a source of well-being and regeneration for humankind – 'Heaven help you all and give you ice and granite'.

But for Muir perhaps the most momentous occurrence of the decade was his 1874 meeting with the Strentzel family at Jeanne Carr's home. Dr and Mrs Strentzel, Polish immigrants and large landowners in the Alhambra Valley of California, had a daughter,

Louie Wanda, whom Jeanne Carr had long wished to introduce to her protégé John Muir. On that day in 1874 they finally met, but it was to be another three years before Muir visited the family and began to take a more than passing interest in the woman who would become his wife. That he did so on his return from a 250-mile river trip on the Merced and San Joaquin, torn and tattered, was typical of Muir. His friend Mary Swett fretted 'that he had made his acquaintance with this girl in such a plight... in a faded greenish-hued coat rather out at the elbows and wrist, his beautiful hair hanging down almost to his shoulders, and I wondered how his appearance had impressed Louie Strentzel'.

She need not have worried. Through the spring of 1878 Muir returned again and again to the Strentzel ranch, he and Louie walked together, and when he travelled away from the Alhambra Valley in 1879, he wrote frequently. On his return to California, he proposed and was accepted. Lying awake, Mrs Strentzel heard her daughter slip into her parents' bedroom and whisper 'All's well, Mother. All's well, and I'm so happy'.

CHAPTER 6

Alaska and marriage

MANY OF MUIR'S FRIENDS WERE astonished – although delighted – that he was to take the plunge. By the time he reached his forties they had marked him down as a perennial bachelor, but he was often lonely in his wanderings and had always cared about family, keeping in close touch with his mother, brothers and sisters. He also had a special affection for children, listening to their woes and telling them stories. When he stayed in the city with his friends the Swetts, the Swett children adopted him, and Cosie Hutchings in old age talked of her 'small child's memories of a patient gentle man holding my sister or myself upon his knee while he showed us the composite parts of flowers ...'.

Fortunately, Nature has a few big places beyond man's power to spoil – the ocean, the two icy ends of the globe, and the Grand Canyon.

Steep Trails, 1918

Although his marriage proposal to Louie had been accepted, he was not yet ready to stay in one place. He had things to do first and those things meant leaving Louie for quite a while. He had spent the summer of 1878 in Utah and Nevada with the US Coast and Geodetic Survey team, and before the wedding took place he wanted to make one more trip, north to Puget Sound in Canada, and, hopefully, on to Alaska.

With his San Francisco friend Thomas Magee, he explored the Sound and then took passage to Alaska on the steamship *California*, in the company of a party of missionaries and their wives intent on converting the local Chilcat Indians. Steaming into Fort Wrangell, the party transferred to the river steamer Cassiar and headed for the Chilcats, but when engine trouble erupted it became apparent that the missionaries' desire to save souls came second to their reluctance to spend more time and money on the trip.

Muir had very little patience with the divines, but he struck up yet another lifelong friendship with the Fort Wrangell resident missionary, S. Hall Young. Together they walked, botanised and climbed. Hall Young, in his *Alaska Days with John Muir*, has given us one of the most graphic – and flattering – descriptions of Muir the mountaineer.

> Muir began to slide up that mountain. I had been with mountain climbers before, but never one like him. A deer lope over the smoother slopes, a sure instinct for the easiest way into a rocky fortress, an instant and unerring attack, a serpent-like glide up the steep; eye, hand and foot all connected dynamically, with no appearance of weight to his body – as though he had Stockton's negative gravity machine strapped on his back.

Muir and Young escaped one afternoon to climb Glenora Peak. Having crossed a glacier and its crevasses, they were nearing the summit when Young fell, dislocating both shoulders and landing with his legs dangling over a 1,000 foot drop. Muir worked his way onto the shelf below his friend, lowered him down by his legs and by holding Young's collar with his teeth, and, cutting footholds as he went, somehow got Young off the mountain. Young tells us that Muir carried him most of the way back to the steamer, stopping to light campfires whenever the injured man's shivering became too great, and resetting one of his shoulders en route.

The senior missionary, Dr Kendall, was not amused when the two exhausted climbers returned, upbraiding Young for his lack of responsibility, but Kendall's wife reacted rather differently. In *Alaska Days with John Muir*, Young tells with delight how she sat on the cabin floor with Young's head in her lap, feeding him coffee from a spoon, while her husband continued to chastise the injured man. 'Then Mrs Kendall turned and thrust her spoon like a sword at him. 'Henry Kendall,' she blazed, 'shut right up and leave this room. Have you no sense? Go instantly, I say!' And the good Doctor went.'

From Young's account, Muir's actions on Glenora became well

known, although Muir did not write about the incident until shortly before his death, when he mentioned it briefly and far more prosaically in his *Travels in Alaska*. Young's attitude towards his friend was reverential – he himself said in *Alaska Days with John Muir* 'I sat at his feet; and at the feet of his spirit I still sit, a student, absorbed, surrendered, as this 'priest of Nature's inmost shrine' unfolds to me the secrets of his 'mountains of God'. But it is Young that we have to thank for many of the Alaskan anecdotes concerning Muir – such as the one where Young was awoken one stormy night by a group of trembling Indians, 'frightened by a mysterious light waving and flickering from the top of the little mountain that overlooked Wrangell'. The supposed 'malignant spirit', Young realises, is 'John Muir, wet but happy, feeding his fire with spruce sticks, studying and enjoying the storm!'

In the autumn Muir received letters from Louie, hoping for his early return – 'So far, so far away, and still another month of wandering in that wild Northland'. Muir would have none of it. 'Leave for the North in a few minutes. Indians waiting. Farewell.' He and Young, with four Indian guides led by Chief Toyatte, set off on a canoe voyage northwards. It was the first time that Muir had come into close contact with the Indians. His brief meetings with them in the Sierra had given him a negative view of the Indian race, but on this trip with Toyatte he realised for the first time how degraded they had become through their contact with white men, separated from their close relationship with the land. They become, he said 'very nearly nothing, lose their wild instincts, and gain a hymnbook, without the means of living'. The Indians admired his courage, naming him the Great Ice Chief, although he frequently infuriated Toyatte by his lack of concern for his own and his companions' safety.

On this trip, too, he saw for the first time the region later named Glacier Bay, a vast expanse of ice and snow, to which he vowed to return. In the meantime, it was back to Fort Wrangell, and Portland, where he delivered 'a snarl of lectures' before returning to California and his long-suffering fiancée.

The marriage took place at the Strentzel family ranch house in Martinez on 14 April 1880, a day of pouring rain. Muir's bride, born in Texas in 1847, had been educated at Miss Atkins Young Ladies Seminary in Benicia, and was a talented pianist. Comparatively little is known about Louie, as, by her own choice, her part in the marriage was very much a supportive one, leaving the limelight to her talkative husband. Graduating from the Seminary in 1864, she had spent the subsequent fifteen years living at her parents' home, not only playing the piano but learning a great deal about the plant life around her and the management of her father's orchards. By the standards of today's independent women, it's too easy to dismiss her as a home-body. That would be unfair and also incorrect. As her father's assistant in the running of his large orchards, she became an able manager and business-woman.

On her marriage to John Muir, she remained mainly at home as she didn't enjoy travel, and certainly had no desire to traverse glaciers, camp out in the woods, or scramble up mountainsides.

Indeed, on the only occasion that she tried it, visiting Yosemite with her husband in 1884, she thoroughly disliked the experience, worrying about bears, tiring easily, and having to be pushed up the steeper slopes by a stout stick wielded by Muir. He sketched the scene, and was irritated by the amount of baggage Louie brought, her need for greater comforts than those provided by the Valley's hotels.

She was a representative woman of her time, and to judge her by today's standards is to take her out of her context. She was a major part of Muir's life and was never far from his thoughts. Although, later on in the marriage, he was often absent from home, he valued her opinion highly, read and reread the early drafts of his books to her, and wrote to her affectionately and frequently.

Louie provided the home base and the comfort which Muir, now in his forties, increasingly felt he needed. The marriage produced two children – Wanda, born 25 March 1881, and Helen, (known as Midge to her father), who arrived on 23 January 1886 – on whom their father doted. Many of his fond letters to them are available in the John Muir papers at the University of the Pacific, in Stockton, California, and a number of his daughter Wanda's letters to him have been published as *Dear Papa: Letters between John Muir and his Daughter Wanda*. All of the letters demonstrate a close and abiding family affection, regardless of time and distance. In her Muir biography, *The Heart of John Muir's World*, Millie Stanley stresses 'what an important part a strong sense of family played in John's life and achievements'. This is true not only of Muir's inherited family – parents and siblings – but also of the one which he chose for himself – Louie, Wanda and Helen, and his parents-in-law, the Strentzels.

When the marriage took place, the Strentzel parents gave their old Dutch colonial-style farmhouse to the newly-weds and built themselves a stately mansion a short distance away at Martinez. The old house in which John and Louie set up home is no longer there, but the mansion is now the John Muir National Historic Site at 4202 Alhambra Avenue, Martinez. When Dr Strentzel died in 1890, the Muirs moved into the big house to be with Mrs Strentzel, and for the remainder of Muir's life it was his home.

The National Historic Site, created in 1964, is open to visitors

The Strenzel/Muir mansion in Martinez

between Wednesday and Sunday, from 10.00 a.m.
to 4.30 p.m. (Tel. 925 228 8860). Completed in
1882, the mansion cost over $20,000 to build
and furnish – a considerable sum at the time
– and incorporated such luxuries as indoor
plumbing and gas lighting. Its seventeen furnished rooms include Muir's and the children's bedrooms, and Muir's restored
'scribble den', where he wrote many of
his best-known works. Structurally,
the house is much as it was in the
Muirs' time, but the area around it
has altered considerably. From
1914 (the year of Muir's death),
the Alhambra orchards began to
decline, squeezed out by the growth of
heavy industry and the demand for build-

Statue of John Muir in the
town of Martinez,
Northern California

ing land. By the 1960s there was almost no farmland left and the
mansion itself was threatened by urban development, a threat
which led ultimately to the foundation of the National Historic
Site in 1964.

Martinez, the county seat of Contra Costa County, was in
Muir's day a flourishing commercial and railroad town, from
where the Strentzels and the Muirs shipped their fruit to the
remainder of the US. It lies thirty two miles north east of San
Francisco and twenty three miles east of Oakland. From
Sacramento/Vallejo, take Highway 80 South, then Highway 4
East, exiting on Alhambra Avenue to Martinez. If you're travelling
from San Francisco/Oakland, take Highway 80 North, then
Highway 4 East, again exiting on Alhambra Avenue; or you can
use Highway 24 to 680 North, and Highway 4 West, exiting on
Alhambra as above.

It's intriguing to wonder whether Muir was ever entirely comfortable in the big house, with its marble fireplaces and twelve foot
high ceilings. It was his father-in-law's style, not his. Perhaps this
question is best answered by the fact that, following the earthquake of 1906, he took the opportunity to replace a damaged

The old adobe ranch house

marble fireplace in the east parlour with a large brick structure which would accommodate 'a real mountain campfire'. Obvious Muir imports, too, are the William Keith paintings which adorn a number of the walls.

In the garden of the mansion is an old Spanish adobe, where, in later years, Muir's daughter Wanda lived with her husband and children. With its traditional construction of sun-dried brick, it seems more in keeping with Muir's concepts of simple living, and towards the end of his life it became one of his favourite places.

Nearby is the Mount Wanda area, administered by the National Park Service, and open seven days a week, sunrise to sunset. Covering 325 acres, it was opened to the public in 1993, and encompasses a part of the original ranch which Muir and his two daughters particularly loved to visit. The two highest points in the park are named after Wanda and Helen, and you can reach it via the 'Park and Ride' area on Franklin Canyon Road and Alhambra Avenue – which also gives access to the Muir Nature Trail.

Also in Martinez is the site where Muir lies buried, in the Strentzel family graveyard on land which was formerly part of the ranch. Staff at the National Historic Site will give you directions to the plot. The pear orchard around it was planted by Dr Strentzel, and alongside John Muir lies Louie, both headstones surmounted by a thistle, the national emblem of Muir's beloved Scotland. Other members of the Strentzel family also lie here, as does Wanda Muir, who died in 1942, and her husband, Thomas Rae Hanna, who followed her in 1947.

A number of visitors to the gravesite have expressed surprise that Muir is buried here, in a conventional plot surrounded by tall iron railings, rather than in the mountains of the Sierra or in the pioneer cemetery of Yosemite Valley. They feel that he should fittingly lie alongside other Yosemite explorers such as the first Guardian of Yosemite, Galen Clark, whose grave can be found in the Valley. This emotion is understandable, given Muir's 'one-ness' with the mountains, but it ignores the fact that he was also very much a family man and that he clearly expressed a wish to be buried here, next to the person who was his partner in marriage and parenthood. Because he was – and is – such a public figure, a hero to many, the public wanted to claim him, to raise a monument in a national park, forgetting that he was also, by choice, a very private man.

The man who said 'the harder the toil, the sweeter the rest', never was profoundly tired.

Stickeen, 1909

From the time of his marriage Muir leased part of the ranch from Dr Strentzel, and on the doctor's death he took over the whole operation, working for long hours in the orchards, providing for his new family, and gradually amassing such a tidy bank balance that he no longer needed to worry about his finances. He and Louie had an agreement that during the pre-harvest ripening period each year, he should be free to visit the wilderness. In late July of that first year of marriage, he set off again for Fort Wrangell, from where he and Young embarked with an Indian crew for Alaska's Sum Dum Bay. Young was astounded to see him back in Wrangell so soon after the wedding – 'What does this

John Muir's Martinez scribble den

mean? Where's your wife?' – but gladly went along. They found and named Young Glacier, sailed up Stephens Passage and over Cross Sound, and towards the end of the voyage discovered what is now called Muir Glacier.

Camping near Taylor Glacier, Muir crept away early one stormy morning on his own, followed by Young's little dog, Stickeen. Muir had objected at the outset to the dog's presence on the canoe trip, suspecting he would become a hindrance, and now he tried to cajole the little 'muggins' to stay in the shelter of the tent. Stickeen could not be dissuaded, so the two set off into the storm, climbing, exploring the glacier, 'tracing the edges of tremendous transverse and longitudinal crevasses, many of which were from twenty to thirty feet wide, and perhaps a thousand feet deep – beautiful and awful'.

Throughout the day, Stickeen kept pace with his hero, despite the fact that the ice continually cut his feet. Muir tied handkerchiefs around his paws, but on the return journey in the fast-growing dusk they came to a crevasse measuring 'about fifty feet' in width, the only route to safety being a 'sliver-bridge' which looped between the two crevasse walls. From his adventure with the little dog, Muir wrote *Stickeen: The Story of a Dog*, in which he explains the nature of this sliver-bridge. Created as the crevasse widened,

> the sliver crossing diagonally was about seventy feet long; its thin knife-edge near the middle was depressed twenty-five or thirty feet below the level of the glacier, and the upcurving ends were attached to the sides eight or ten feet below the brink.

Muir tells us that, seeing no alternative, he cuts steps and notches in the near bank, climbs down onto the sliver-bridge and edges across, 'keeping my balance with my knees pressed against the sides. The tremendous abyss on either hand I studiously ignored'. Eventually reaching safety on the far side, he can't believe he's accomplished the crossing : 'the thing seemed to have been done by somebody else'. To the reader, the task seems impossible, its success difficult to believe. (Is Muir indulging in a little embroidery here?) Even more so are Stickeen's subsequent actions. Desperate at the possibility of being abandoned on the ice, he eventually

When I heard the storm and looked out I made haste to join it ...

Stickeen, 1909

works up the courage to slide his feet down into the first notch, 'bunching all four in it and almost standing on his head'. Slowly, oh so slowly, he makes his way across the sliver-bridge to the foot of the climb on Muir's side. 'Here he halted in dead silence, and it was here I feared he might fail, for dogs are poor climbers.' But the brave little dog makes it to the top and goes mad with joy at his deliverance, whirling around Muir like a dervish.

Muir never forgot him – 'I have known many dogs, and many a story I could tell of their wisdom and devotion; but to none do I owe so much as to Stickeen' – and the dog's behaviour confirmed his belief that animals have emotions and powers of reasoning very similar to those of human beings. By writing *Stickeen* he ensured that his companion on that icy adventure will never be forgotten.

Back at the ranch in Martinez, Wanda was born in March

1881, to adoring parents and grandparents. Muir continued to work long hours in the orchards, but the never-ending work round, and the absence from his beloved mountains and wilderness, began to take its toll. He was often short-tempered, developed a hacking cough, and lost weight rapidly. Louie was worried about him and, in May 1881, less than two months after the birth of their daughter, she selflessly persuaded him to join the cutter Thomas Corwin, en route to the Bering Strait to search for the steamer Jeannette, which had left for the Arctic in 1879 and had vanished without a trace. Muir and his companions explored Herald Island and Wrangel Land, but found no Jeannette survivors (most of the crew perished on the ice, the remnants eventually reaching Siberia).

Returning to the Alhambra Valley, Muir spent the subsequent years running the Martinez ranch, escaping when he could from his farmer's cares to the high country. In the summer of 1883 he had a visit from Young, who tells us Muir described himself as 'condemned to penal servitude with these miserable little bald-heads (holding up a bunch of cherries). Boxing them up; putting them in prison! And for money! Man! I'm like to die of the shame of it'. He camped at Lake Tahoe with Charles C. Parry; and, in July 1888, he and William Keith visited Oregon and Washington, where Muir climbed Mount Rainier He wrote to Louie, 'Did not mean to climb it, but got excited, and soon was on top'.

In the Oregon forests, he was appalled at the devastation wrought by lumbering during the years he had been immersed in ranching. But, at the same time, his journals and letters home took on a note of rapture, a renewed sense of wonder in the beauty of the woods. Louie, seeing all too clearly the difference between his ill health and overwork in Martinez, and the contrasting euphoria and energy which came to him in the wilderness, wrote to him on 9 August 1888:

> A ranch that needs and takes the sacrifice of a noble life, or work, ought to be flung away beyond all reach and power for harm ... . The Alaska book and the Yosemite book, dear John, must be written, and you need to be your own self, well and strong, to make them worthy of you. There is nothing that has a right to be considered beside this except the wel-

fare of our children.

And Louie meant what she said. It would take a year or more to make alternative arrangements for managing the ranch, but Muir from this date gradually withdrew from farm management.

In the meantime, he had had no meeting with his father since that acrimonious parting at Hickory Hill back in 1867. Daniel Muir had moved to Canada, where for eight years he worked with the Disciples of Christ in Hamilton, Ontario. A bad fall on an icy pavement left him with a damaged hip, and he moved south again, living with his favourite daughter Joanna, and her husband Walter Brown, in Arkansas. Here, following the birth of Joanna's first child, he became a doting grandfather and confided to his daughter that he regretted the harsh treatment he had meted out to his own children.

In the late summer of 1885, John Muir had his second premonition, a feeling that if he didn't reach his father immediately, it would be too late. He hurried to Arkansas, and when Daniel Muir died, in early October, seven of his eight children were with him, his eldest son holding his hand. Whatever the confrontations and differences of the past, John put them aside when he wrote

John and Louie's gravestones

Daniel's obituary: 'His life was singularly clean and pure. He never had a single vice excepting, perhaps, the vices over over-industry and over-giving... . He loved little children, and beneath a stern face, rigid with principle, he carried a warm and tender heart'.

During the summer of 1889, Muir accompanied Robert Underwood Johnson, editor of the *Century*, on a trip to Yosemite. Fired by Muir's enthusiasm and his despair at the way in which grazing animals were destroying the glacial meadows, Johnson determined to support the creation of Yosemite as a national park. With this in mind, he asked Muir to write two articles for the *Century*, one setting out the threat to Yosemite, the other suggesting the area to be included in the proposed park. Muir was sceptical as to whether his pleas would have any affect, but there was the precedent of Yellowstone, which had been created a national park in 1872. He wrote the articles.

'Treasures of the Yosemite' was published in the August 1890 *Century*, followed by 'Features of the Proposed Yosemite National Park', while the powerful voice of Johnson lobbied in Washington and New York. The Yosemite Bill was introduced in Congress; on 30 September 1890 it passed both Houses, and was signed into law the following day by President Harrison. Now Yosemite could be protected by cavalry patrols, with graziers being turned back at the borders; but Yosemite Valley was not included, remaining under the jurisdiction of the State of California.

The Bill's passage had not been achieved without a considerable degree of mud-slinging by Muir's opponents. John P. Irish, writing in the *Oakland Tribune*, accused Muir of hypocrisy in pleading the cause of conservation while cutting timber during his Yosemite employment with Hutchings. Muir hotly refuted the charge, publishing a denial in the 14 September 1890 *Tribune*, but the accusation was a forerunner to many others which would be directed at Muir. As his fame grew and his conservation battles intensified, so those who stood to lose by his intervention – notably the farming and timber industries – became increasingly hostile. John Muir was now public property, and as such was fair game.

CHAPTER 7

The public Muir

WITH A GROWING PUBLIC AWARENESS of the need for preservation of wild places, Muir and a small band of friends – Johnson and Warren Olney prominent among them – formed the Sierra Club, whose stated aims were

> To explore, enjoy and render accessible the mountain regions of the Pacific Coast; to publish authentic information concerning them; to enlist the support and co-operation of the people and the government in preserving the forests and other natural features of the Sierra Nevada Mountains.

The Club was formed in 1892, with Muir as President-for-life, and its first success was the defeat of a proposal to drastically reduce the area covered by the new Yosemite National Park. The Sierra Club effectively mobilised opposition on behalf of conservation, a function which they have been fulfilling ever since. With headquarters in San Francisco, regional offices, legal advisors, and a publishing section, the Club today has one of the largest Congressional lobbying operations in the US, plugging away at persuading legislators to preserve wild areas. Its membership exceeds 600,000, and it has a vast 'outings' programme which includes not only local US activities but also international trips to places such as Muir's birthplace in Scotland. Muir was active in many of the first Sierra Club trips into Yosemite, and a number of the old photographs held in the Muir collection at the University of the Pacific, Stockton, California, show him out in the woods surrounded by early Club members.

When we try to pick out anything by itself, we find it hitched to everything else in the Universe.

My First Summer in the Sierra, 1911

Muir continued to worry away at the writing, which he never found easy, needing complete quiet to aid the creative process. When he was in his 'scribble den', Louie and the two girls would tiptoe about, and piano playing took place in a sound-proof room at the opposite end of the house.

He was also preoccupied with family matters. When Dr Strentzel died in October 1890, the Muirs moved into the big house and John took over the estate management. He was greatly helped in this by his sister and brother-in-law, Maggie and John Reid, who moved to Martinez to shoulder part of the work of overseeing the ranch. In March 1892, when his brother David's Portage firm went bankrupt, David and his wife Juliette joined the Martinez ranch, working on a profit-sharing basis.

By 1893, the knowledge that the farm was in good hands gave Muir the confidence to accompany William Keith and his wife on a long planned European tour. Stopping off in Portage to spend time with his mother, he visited the World's Columbian Exposition in Chicago, and was fêted by society when he paused in New York to see Robert Underwood Johnson. So long did he pause that the Keiths left for Europe without him. He followed in late June.

This was his first trip 'home' to Scotland since he had left as a boy of eleven, and he wanted to see everything, everyone. He visited Edinburgh, and Dunbar, where he saw again the homes of his youth and the Davel Brae school, climbed the Lammermuir Hills, and walked and talked with his favourite cousin, Margaret Lunam. Saddened by the poverty which still existed in Dunbar, he later sent Margaret a Christmas draft for distribution to the poor, a habit he maintained for the rest of his life. And he wrote glowingly to his two daughters of the beauty of Scotland and his desire to camp out in the blooming heather.

Next came Norway, the Lake District in August, London (which he thoroughly disliked – not surprisingly, for a lover of the wilderness), Switzerland and Italy's Lake Como, then back to London for a visit to Kew Gardens (which he *did* like), and on to Ireland's Killarney Lakes. There was a final return to Scotland's north east, and then home to California, making a brief stop in New York to further plead the cause of conservation.

The Mountains of California, a compilation of articles written for the *Century*, came out in 1894 and was an immediate success. It was Muir's first full-length published book, and the acclaim with which it was greeted inspired him to labour on with the writing. While working in June 1896 he felt a portent of his mother's death and hurried to Portage. In her son's presence she rallied, but died shortly afterwards.

In July of the same year, under pressure from Johnson and Charles S. Sargent (an American forestry expert), a fact-finding National Forestry Commission was appointed to examine the affect of commercial interests on the west's trees. The Commission, accompanied by Muir, inspected areas in South Dakota, Wyoming, Washington, Oregon, and points south.

In Montana, Gifford Pinchot, also a commissioner, joined the group. A young European-trained forester, he had gained prominence for his work in restricting eastern lumbering. He and Muir, with apparently similiar conservation aims, became friends, little knowing that they were later to become fierce opponents, particularly in the battle for the beautiful valley of the Hetch Hetchy. The Commission worked its way southward through California to Arizona, where Muir and Pinchot viewed the wonders of the Grand Canyon from an unconventional standpoint – upsidedown: 'standing with our heads down brought out the colours – reds, grays, ashy greens of varied limestones and sandstones, lavender, and tones nameless and numberless'.

The compromise Commission report (with which Pinchot disagreed) found that damage to the forests was widespread and devastating – notably by sheep farming, lumbering and railroad incursions. The report suggested the creation of thirteen forest reserves, with a ban on sheep grazing, to be policed by the military. The outgoing President Cleveland signed these reserves, totalling twenty one million acres, into being, and all hell broke loose. Throughout the west, commercial interests and small farmers alike vehemently opposed the legislation, seeing it as an infringement of their god-given right to help themselves to timber where and whenever they wished. Outrage was so widespread that the Presidential order was suspended until March 1898.

The beleaguered Muir found an avenue by which to counter-act this outburst. For Walter Hines Page of the *Atlantic Monthly* he wrote a series of articles on forest preservation. The first of these, 'The American Forests', appeared in the August 1897 issue, and in it Muir cut directly to the heart of the matter. 'Any fool can destroy trees. They cannot run away; and if they could, they would still be destroyed – chased and hunted down as long as fun or a dollar could be got out of their bark hides, branching horns, or magnificent bole backbones ... . Through all the wonderful, eventful centuries since Christ's time – and long before that – God has cared for these trees ... but he cannot save them from fools – only Uncle Sam can do that.'

While in Seattle, Muir read of Gifford Pinchot's statement that sheep grazing in reserves did no harm. In a hotel lobby, he accosted and questioned Pinchot, who confirmed his statement, resulting in a permanent rift between the two men. From this time onwards, the fledgling conservation movement was split into the 'preserva-tionists' such as Muir, who sought to protect the land, not only for its beauty and inspirational value to man but also for its own sake, and the utilitarian 'conservationists', whose views are neatly encapsulated in one of Pinchot's statements. 'The object of our forest policy is not to preserve the forests because they are beautiful or wild or the habitat of wild animals; it is to ensure a steady supply of timber for human prosperity. Every other consideration comes as secondary.'

This 'managed care' of the wilderness for man's benefit was anathema to Muir and his like. Since those first journal entries on his long walk to the Gulf, he had continued to speak out against the use by mankind of all living things, and yet here was the man-aged care argument being used in the name of conservation.

In the spring of 1898 he travelled again, in the company of friends Charles Sargent and William Canby, this time to the deep South, which was still suffering from the long-lasting affects of the Civil War. In Florida, he sought out elderly Mrs Hodgson, who had nursed him back to health from malarial fever all those years ago, then continued on to New York and Montreal.

In May of the following year he joined the Harriman

Expedition to Alaska. (During these years of the 'public Muir', the patient Louie must have occasionally forgotten what her husband looked like.) The railway magnate, E. H. Harriman, advised by his doctor to take a rest from business, invited over one hundred eminent scientists of various disciplines on a research trip to the fiords and glaciers of Alaska. On board the *George W. Elder*, they steamed from Portland to Glacier Bay, Prince William Sound, Kodiak Island, and across the stormy Bering Sea to St. Lawrence Island. At first, Muir was wary of Harriman, who seemed to embody the commercialism which Muir so abhorred, but during the journey he changed his opinion and the two men remained friends until Harriman's death in 1909. On Muir's world tours, Harriman offered him free passage on his steamship lines, and after Harriman's death Muir wrote an appreciation of the railway king – *Edward Henry Harriman*, published in 1911.

John Burroughs, one of America's foremost nature writers and an old friend and sparring partner of Muir's – they were known to their friends as 'the two Johnnies' – was also a member of the expedition. Muir had convinced him that the Bering Sea would be 'like a millpond', and when (of course) it was rough, Burroughs, prostrate on his bunk, turned to acid doggerel.

> Had not John Muir put in his lip
> Thou hadst not found me in this ship,
> Groaning on my narrow bed,
> Heaping curses on thy head ...

Back home, things were far more serious. In 1901 the city of San Francisco put forward a proposal to build a reservoir in the Hetch Hetchy Valley, while Muir and the Sierra Club began to campaign against the idea. In September 1901 President McKinley was shot in Buffalo, dying on 13 September, and on the following day Theodore Roosevelt was sworn in as President. On his first message to Congress in December of that year, he declared forest preservation to be 'an imperative business necessity' and recommended the creation of a Bureau of Forestry.

Roosevelt came into office determined to stamp out abuses and support conservation. In early 1903 he requested a visit to the west and a meeting with John Muir. Muir, who had a long-standing arrangement to accompany Charles Sargent on a European and Asian tour, was dubious about disappointing Sargent. Learning of his hesitation, Roosevelt wrote to Muir 'I do not want anyone with me but you, and I want to drop politics absolutely for four days, and just be out in the open with you'. Muir, of course, postponed his travel plans, and Sargent wrote back, accepting his decision but making a number of uncomplimentary statements about the President and his high-handed ways.

In May, on meeting the President, Muir handed Sargent's letter to him, intending only to demonstrate how he had shelved other activities to accommodate the meeting, and forgetting, in typical Muir fashion, that the letter contained comments for his eyes only. Once Roosevelt started to read, Muir of course recalled its contents and tried to snatch it back, much to the President's amusement. It was not an auspicious beginning, but was to be the only hiccup in their time together. Camping out in Yosemite – in the Mariposa Grove, at Glacier Point, and in Bridalveil meadow – they eluded the press and the planned entertainments, and spent three days and nights talking, talking, talking. Roosevelt loved camping out – 'This is bully', he roared to his guide – and became imbued with Muir's desire that each generation should inherit the wilderness.

It seems strange that a paper that reads smoothly and may be finished in ten minutes should require months to write.

Journal entry written at Martinez,
6 February 1895

Feeling confident that the cause of conservation would now be furthered at Presidential level, Muir eventually left for his world trip with the Sargents in late May. He saw little that he admired in Europe, enjoyed the Russian forests and disliked St Petersburg (well, he was never at home in any city), where he became ill and had to be stretchered onto his train. Siberia was followed by Manchuria and ptomaine poisoning. Hoping for a return to health, he parted from the Sargents and visited the great Himalayas – which he felt himself too old and too unwell to climb – followed by the Egyptian pyramids.

Throughout the trip he had a sense of foreboding that all was not well at home. The health of his younger daughter, Helen, had always been at risk, and he worried constantly about her. Eventually he succeeded in contacting Louie and, reassured that his fears were ungrounded, he embarked on the final phase of the journey, which reads like a Cook's Tour of the Orient and the South Seas – Australia, New Zealand, the Phillipines, China, Japan, Honolulu. The passage home was by courtesy of Harriman on his steamship *Siberia*, and Muir finally reached San Francisco and his family in late May, over a year after leaving home.

In his absence, the Sierra Club (backed, behind the scenes, by Harriman's powerful Southern Pacific Railroad lobby) had continued to fight for the inclusion of Yosemite Valley in the National Park. The Valley had remained within the jurisdiction of the State of California, and commercial interests continued to make inroads on its forests and meadows. Muir and the Sierra Club wanted it under Federal control, which would halt the incursions, and their efforts were rewarded in June 1906, when the Valley formally became part of Yosemite National Park. The battle had lasted seventeen years, with Muir playing no small part in the fight, as public opinion had moved increasingly behind the conservationists since the publication of his *Our National Parks* in 1901.

In an attempt to have the Grand Canyon protected in the same way, he wrote 'The Grand Canyon of the Colorado' (later included in *Steep Trails*, published by his literary executor in 1918), in which he rejoices that

> nature has a few big places beyond man's power to spoil – the ocean, the two icy ends of the globe, and the Grand Canyon ... It is a vast wilderness of rocks in a sea of light, coloured and glowing like oak and maple woods in autumn, when the sun-gold is richest.

In 1908 Roosevelt, prodded by Muir, accorded National Monument status to the eight hundred thousand acres of the Canyon, and it was eventually made a full National Park in 1919.

Muir felt that 'it is impossible to learn what the Canyon is like from descriptions and pictures', a comment supported by just about everyone who has visited it. This gigantic hole in the ground fractures the Colorado Plateau for over two hundred miles, measuring up to eighteen miles from rim to rim, and attracts over three million visitors a year, mostly in July and August. The park now covers two thousand square miles and includes hundreds of smaller canyons and dozens of buttes, with a two hundred and ten mile drive between the two rims. Recent research dates the inner gorges at over two billion years old, while the buttes close to the rims are around two hundred million, the Canyon itself a mere few million years in age. Colin Fletcher, a dedicated hiker of wild places, walked from end to end of the Canyon in 1963 and called the journal of his trip *The Man Who Walked Through Time*, because of the geological time frame through which he passed.

In many places on the rim you can stand on the very edge of the chasm and look down, and down, and down, your eyes focusing and refocusing into the unexpected depth – 'the verge anywhere, everywhere', said Muir, 'is a point of interest beyond one's wildest dreams'. And the colours! Reds, golds, blue and violet, orange, ochre, umber, pinks and purples on the Canyon walls, on distant mesas and buttes, with ant like figures hiking the Bright Angel Trail thousands of feet below. At dawn and at sunset it's a photographer's mecca, as the changing light alters the shape and hue of the rock faces and the evening deepens to blue and purple twilight. There's also a wide temperature variation. It may be below freezing at the rim, particularly on the higher elevations of the North Rim, whereas in the Canyon bottom summer temperatures routinely register over 100F. If you hike down into the Canyon, heed the rangers' warnings to calculate 'one minute down, two minutes up'. Usually you climb *up* a mountain first, stopping when it becomes over-strenuous, and doing the easier bit, descending, when you're tired. In the Canyon this process is reversed and it's all too easy to overstretch yourself and forget that you're not simply walking back, you're climbing up several thousand feet.

Don't be put off by the seasonal bustle of the South Rim's Village. Do what Muir did. Walk a short distance away from any of the main trails and points of interest and you'll find yourself alone with the Canyon. He went

> quietly afoot along the rim at different times of day and night, free to observe the vegetation, the fossils in the rocks, the seams beneath overhanging ledges once inhabited by Indians, and to watch the stupendous scenery in the changing lights and shadows, clouds, showers and storms.

Or, if you want to leave the crowds altogether, get yourself to the North Rim, around twelve miles away as the crow flies but a two hundred and ten mile drive around the perimeter, and a thousand feet higher than the South Rim. North Rim is accessible from May to October, when the snow melts, is visited by far fewer tourists, and offers stunning views from a number of trails such as the Bright Angel Point Trail, which leads you for a quarter of a mile along a narrow bridge between two heart-stopping chasms.

To reach the South Rim, you can fly into nearby Flagstaff, there's also a small Canyon airport, and numerous US tour operators offer inclusive trips. From the town of Williams you can ride the old steam train to the Canyon – book early, especially during the summer months. The park lies north of Interstate 40, and, as you would expect for one of the world's wonders, is amply signposted. To reach the South Rim from Williams, drive north on Highway 64; from Flagstaff take Highway 180, which joins Highway 64 south of the park.

To access the North Rim, you need Highway 67 south into the park. Highway 67 is reached via Highway 89, from Flagstaff in the south, via Bitter Springs or Page. From the north, take the Highway 9 exit from Interstate 15, in Utah (marked Zion National Park). Highway 9 connects with Highway 89 at Kanab, then Highway 67 to the North Rim.

For information on the Canyon, you can write to Grand Canyon National Park, PO Box 129, Grand Canyon, Arizona 86023 (Tel. 520 638 7888), or access their web page at *www/thecanyon.com/nps*.

Muir and the Sierra Club had been successful in preserving Yosemite Valley, but for Muir, things were not going so well on the home front. Helen, always frail, suffered several bouts of pneumonia, and the doctor prescribed the clean, dry air of the desert. In 1905, while Louie remained at Martinez as usual, John and Wanda took Helen to the Sierra Bonita Ranch, near Wilcox, Arizona. There, a telegram reached them, urging an immediate return to Louie's bedside. She had a tumour on the lung and lived only until 9 August that year. Dazed and unbelieving, Muir buried his wife in the Strentzel family plot before returning to the desert, at Adamana, Arizona. The next year passed in a haze of grief, during which he endured a period of 'mental barrenness' and wrote nothing.

He found two comforts, two ways of making life livable during this time of mourning. Wanda and Helen were with him at the Forest Hotel, six miles north of what is known as the Petrified Forest, and soon Helen grew stronger, riding further each day with her sister, sleeping in a tent, despite often freezing desert nights, to take full advantage of that clear desert air.

Petrified wood

Secondly, near Adamana are two areas of great beauty and scientific interest – the Painted Desert and the Petrified Forest – in which Muir increasingly spent his days. The Painted Desert area is composed of many-coloured badlands, where the changing light gives the land an ever-fluctuating range of hues, while the Petrified Forest consists of thousands of fossilised trees from the Triassic period, over 160 million years ago. The petrified logs, embedded with the plants and small animals of long ago, have the appearance of stone, with glowing colours and crystal-like patterns.

Muir was fascinated by the petrified wood, and discovered the Blue Forest – now called the Blue Mesa and included in Petrified Forest National Park. You can visit the park, created in 1962, anytime of the year within daylight hours, and see the ancient wood which so intrigued John Muir and helped him through a time of grief. The park's 93,533 acres include areas of the Painted Desert and lie between Interstate 40 and Highway 180. If travelling west on Interstate 40, exit at Milepost 311 to drive through the park, connecting with US 180 at the south end. You can then pick up US 180 west to Holbrook and back onto Interstate 40 west. If you're eastbound, exit Interstate 40 at Holbrook to take US 180 east to the park, driving north through the park to rejoin Interstate 40 east.

At the time of the Muirs' stay, the Petrified Forest had no protection, and many of its logs were being carted away for sale, its precious fossils being chipped out by souvenir hunters. Horrified at the decimation, Muir and others persuaded Congressman John F. Lacey to propose legislation which would protect areas of historic and scientific value. In 1906, under the Lacey Antiquities Act, President Roosevelt set aside what would later become the Petrified Forest National Monument, followed in 1908 by similiar legislation to preserve the Grand Canyon.

When Helen was judged well enough, there was a return to Martinez. Wanda, married in 1906 to Thomas Rae Hanna, set up home in the old adobe ranch-house, and Muir and Helen settled into the big house, now achingly empty with just the two of them and their Chinese manservant. Helen appeared cured, but in time her hacking cough returned, and in 1907 her doctor again prescribed desert air, this time for a minimum of two years. Her father took her to Daggett, California, in the Mojave Desert, made sure she was comfortably housed, engaging a companion for her and transporting her dog and pony, and returned sadly to Martinez.

Muir had hoped that in time Helen would be able to return to northern California, but her health improved so dramatically in the desert that she remained there, marrying Buel Funk, a member of a local ranching family, giving birth to four sons, and living into her late seventies. The small town of Daggett hasn't changed dramatically since Muir's day, with its population still under one thousand. It lies to the south east of Barstow, bypassed by

None of Nature's landscapes are ugly so long as they are wild.

Our National Parks, 1901

Interstate 40. Helen's house out at the Van Dyke Ranch is still standing, as is Desertaire, the house built by the Funks after Muir's death.

Meanwhile, in October 1907, fellow-Scots Muir and William Keith had taken the opportunity to camp out in the Sierra, including a visit to Hetch Hetchy. The 1906 San Francisco earthquake and subsequent fire had increased the city's determination to find a reliable source of water – and hydro-electricity – and mayor James D.Phelan had made an application to build a reservoir in Hetch Hetchy Valley. The application was refused by Hitchcock, Roosevelt's Secretary of the Interior, in spite of a San Francisco city appeal direct to Roosevelt. By this time Gifford Pinchot, Muir's adversary, was the President's Chief Forester, and when Hitchcock was succeeded by James Garfield, a friend and sup-porter of Pinchot's, the future of Hetch Hetchy did not look good.

At the same time, a Conservation Conference took place at the White House, convened by Roosevelt and Pinchot, at which dis-cussion centred around the use of raw resources rather than the preservation of wilderness for leisure and future generations. Muir and other major conservationists were not invited. In early 1909 President Taft succeeded Roosevelt and hearings took place on the Hetch Hetchy dam project. Feelings and debate ran high, with James D. Phelan slandering Muir, saying that Muir would 'sacrifice his own family for the preservation of beauty'.

Later that year, the new President visited Yosemite in Muir's company. Unlike Roosevelt's visit to Yosemite, there was no camp-ing, no fireside chats, but a Presidential train and constant press reporting. Taft teased Muir by saying that the Hetch Hetchy Valley entrance would make a good dam. Muir, becoming more and more beleaguered as the long fight for the Valley wore on, did not laugh – '... the man who would dam that would be damning himself!' Following the visit, government engineers concluded that damming Lake Eleanor would be sufficient and Hetch Hetchy would not be needed. Muir and the Sierra Club felt quietly opti-mistic.

But it was not to be. When the country went to the polls in 1912, it chose a Democrat, Woodrow Wilson, whose new

Secretary, Franklin K. Lane, favoured the Hetch Hetchy reservoir plan. Eventually, the Raker Bill, giving the city of San Francisco the use of Hetch Hetchy, was signed into law by Woodrow Wilson in early December 1913.

The battle for the Valley had monopolised Muir's thoughts and time for over six years, had caused bitter conflict within the ranks of the conservationists, and had considerably slowed Muir's literary output. By 1913 he was seventy five years old – more importantly, he *felt* old, old and tired, dispirited, betrayed. It would have been all too easy for him to have remained that way, to have retreated into bitterness and disillusionment. A number of his close friends were no longer there to cheer him – Harriman had died in 1909, William Keith in 1911 – and he must have felt very much isolated by the defeat of 1913, alone in the big house in Martinez, at odds with the progress of public policy.

But he pulled himself away from the bitterness, the retreat, and became instead the grand old man of American conservation – he became a national icon. Honorary degrees were showered upon him, places named in his honour, the public clamoured to meet him, to shake his hand. One of the 'namings' which pleased him most was the 1907 gift to the nation by William Kent of a forty seven acre section of redwoods – to be named, by Kent's request, the Muir Woods National Monument. Muir's autobiography of the early years, *The Story of My Boyhood and Youth*, had been published in serial form during 1912 and 1913, and although its graphic descriptions of beatings had shocked many readers, the public felt that because they now shared in his upbringing, they knew him, that John Muir was somehow theirs.

He had, too, the memories of the journey he had made in 1911 and 1912 to South America and Africa, a trip for which he had yearned and planned since he was a young lad in Wisconsin. Surprisingly for a man who seemed most at home in the snow and ice of the high Sierra and the Alaskan glaciers, he also had a need for the tropics. 'For many a year I have been impelled towards the Lord's tropic gardens of the South. Many influences have tended to blunt or bury this constant longing, but it has outlived and overpowered them all.' In August 1911 he had finally sailed up the

Amazon, just as in his boyhood dream, to see the river's giant water lilies, explored deep into the rain forest, and gone in search of the monkey puzzle tree in the Chilean Andes. In Africa, he travelled from Cape Town to Victoria Falls, although he was far more interested in the Zambezi baobab forests than in any cities or tourist attractions. 'Kings may be blest, but I am glorious! Wandered about in the woods that fringe the Falls, dripping with spray, and through the Baobab woods'.

In those final years, he had so many good friends who cosseted him and made him welcome. Escaping from the winter fogs of northern California, he spent some time in Pasadena, and in Los Angeles where the J. D. Hooker family always made him welcome. An anecdote related by his friend Calkins, and quoted in Linnie Marsh Wolfe's biography of John Muir, demonstrates how little his fame had affected him.

> John D. Hooker's big car and chauffeur arrived to carry him to the Hooker home in Los Angeles for a visit, so he went up to his room to pack. Presently he came down the stately stairway, carrying a shabby, old-fashioned satchel that had come open at one end. Behind him for several feet trailed an exceedingly long gray nightgown of the old school, a wide, woolen flood, cascading down from step to step. His host and hostess and other guests, standing below to bid him farewell, began to show signs of mirth. Glancing back he saw the nightgown. But he was not disturbed, and saw no need for explanation or apology. He simply said: 'Ha! I seem to be losing some of my gear', set the satchel down in the midst of the company and proceeded to reel in the vagrant gown, stowing it in by handfuls well-thrust home, utterly unconscious that he was even remotely amusing.

When the First World War broke out in the summer of 1914, Muir, by nature opposed to the very idea of military conflict, was deeply distressed. Feeling physically and emotionally drained, he attempted to bury himself in the editing of his journals for *Travels in Alaska*, with the assistance of Marion Randall Parsons, one of the leading lights of the Sierra Club. He also modernised the Martinez mansion, installing electricity and new furnishings.

In June Helen had presented him with another grandson,

whom he had not yet seen, and shortly before Christmas he decided to pay a visit to Daggett. On the journey there he felt a cold coming on, but walked in the desert with Helen and worked on the book manuscript. Within twenty four hours he became obviously ill and the doctors diagnosed pneumonia. Transported the eighty miles to the California Hospital in Los Angeles, he was admitted shortly before midnight on 23 December, and the next morning seemed to have improved. The improvement was short-lived and he died on Christmas Eve 1914.

Back in 1865, writing to Jeanne Carr from Trout Hollow in Canada, Muir had said 'A lifetime is so little a time that we die ere we get ready to live'. Into his own 'little time' he had packed a wealth of activities – brother, husband, father, farmer, inventor, naturalist, mountaineer, writer, conservationist, but, most importantly to him, lover of all living things.

John Muir Chronology

1838   John Muir born 21 April, at 128 High Street, Dunbar, Scotland

1839   The Muir family move to 130-134 High Street, Dunbar

1841   Enters Davel Brae primary school

1845   Enters Dunbar Grammar School

1849   Daniel Muir, with three children including John, emigrates to Buffalo Township, Wisconsin. Fountain Lake Farm established

1856   Muir family moves from Fountain Lake to Hickory Hill Farm, also in Buffalo Township

1860   John leaves home, exhibits inventions at Madison State Fair. First public recognition in Wisconsin State Journal. Meets Jeanne Carr

1861   Enrolls at University of Wisconsin, Madison. American Civil War begins

1863   Leaves University of Wisconsin

1864   Travels to Canada, discovers *Calypso Borealis*, works for Trout's sawmill/factory in Meaford, Ontario

1866   Trout's mill burns down, Muir moves to Indianapolis, Indiana, where he works in a carriage factory. First published work 'The Calypso Borealis' in *Boston Recorder*

1867   Muir blinded in accident. Sets out on 1,000 mile journey to the Gulf of Mexico

1868   Travels from Cuba via New York and Isthmus of Panama to San Francisco. First visit to Yosemite

1869   Sheep herding in the Californian High Sierra

1870   Lives in Yosemite Valley, working for James Hutchings, begins Yosemite guiding, meets Joseph Le Conte

1871   Ralph Waldo Emerson visits Muir in Yosemite. *New York Tribune* publishes Yosemite Glaciers

1872   The *Overland Monthly* publishes Yosemite Valley in Flood, Twenty Hill Hollow, Living Glaciers of California. Meets Scottish artist William Keith, makes first ascent of Mount Ritter

1873   Makes solo climb of Mount Whitney

1874   Makes solo ascent of Mount Shasta. The *Overland Monthly* starts publishing Muir's *Studies in the Sierra*, meets Louie Wanda Strentzel

1875   Makes ascents of Mount Shasta and Mount Whitney

1876   Gives first public lecture, to Literary Institute of Sacramento. Works for forest preservation and publishes 'God's First Temples' in Sacramento Record-Union

1877   Guides US Geodetic Survey of Nevada and Utah mountains

1878   'The Hummingbird of the California Water Falls' published in *Scribners Monthly*

1879   Becomes engaged to Louie Strentzel. First trip to Alaska, befriends S. Hall Young, discovers Glacier Bay and Muir Glacier

1880   Marries Louie Strentzel, makes second Alaskan trip, adventures with Stickeen

1881   Travels to Alaska aboard the *Corwin*, birth of daughter Wanda Muir

1882   Muir starts period of fruit farming in Martinez

1884   Muir takes Louie to visit Yosemite

1885   Daniel Muir dies

1886   Birth of second daughter, Helen

1888   Travels to Puget Sound and Mount Shasta, climbs Mount Rainier, *Picturesque California* published

1890   Fourth visit to Alaska, Yosemite articles published in Century magazine, Yosemite declared a National Park, Dr Strentzel dies, Muir family moves into Martinez mansion

1892   Muir and friends establish the Sierra Club

1893   European tour, including Scotland

1894   Muir's first full length work, *The Mountains of California*, published

1896   Accompanies US Forestry Commission survey of western forests, fifth visit to Alaska, Anne Gilrye Muir dies

1897   Sixth trip to Alaska, publishes forest preservation articles in *Harper's Weekly* and *Atlantic Monthly*

1898   Visits Southern states, writes *The Wild Parks and Forest Reservations of the West*

1899   Participates in Harriman Expedition, Mount Rainier National Park established

1901   Publishes *Our National Parks*, San Francisco begins campaign to acquire Hetch Hetchy, first Sierra Club annual trip to Yosemite

1903   Spends three days camping with President Roosevelt in Yosemite. World tour to Europe, Asia, Far East, Australia, New Zealand

1905   Campaigns for return of Yosemite Valley to Federal control. Takes daughter Helen to Arizona desert, studies Petrified Forest. Louie Muir dies

1906   Petrified Forest declared National Monument, Yosemite Valley returned to Federal control, Wanda Muir marries, San Francisco earthquake and fire

1907   Campaign starts to save Hetch Hetchy

1908   Grand Canyon and Muir Woods become National Monuments

1909   *Stickeen* published, Muir meets President Taft in the Sierra

1910   Daughter Helen marries

1911   *My First Summer in the Sierra* published, travels to South America and Africa

1912   *The Yosemite* published

1913   Hetch Hetchy granted to San Francisco, *Story of My Boyhood and Youth* published

1914   Christmas Eve, Muir dies in California Hospital, Los Angeles

Afterword

THE INFLUENCE OF JOHN MUIR'S life and work did not cease with his passing, nor did publication of his writings. After his death on Christmas Eve 1914, Marion Randall Parsons completed the editing of *Travels in Alaska* and it was published in 1915 by Muir's literary executor, William Frederic Badè. Badè also edited and published *A Thousand Mile Walk to the Gulf* (1916), *The Cruise of the Corwin* (1917), *Steep Trails* (1918), and *The Life and Letters of John Muir* (1924).

In 1915, *Letters to a Friend* (letters written by John Muir to Jeanne Carr) was issued, and this was followed by Linnie Marsh Wolfe's Pulitzer Prize-winning biography, *Son of the Wilderness: The Life of John Muir* (1945). Wolfe also edited Muir's unpublished journals – *John o' the Mountains: The Unpublished Journals of John Muir* (1938). Since that date, biographies and critical works on Muir have continued to appear at frequent intervals in the United States; there are photographic coffee-table books, children's versions, weighty academic tomes, interpretations of his life from numerous perspectives. You name it, it's probably been written about Muir, such is the continuing interest – notably in the western US – in the man and his achievements.

In the same way, his determination to protect and preserve the wilderness has continued to inspire those who came after him. Robert Moran, the Irish engineer whom Muir befriended on his first steamboat trip to Alaska, later donated 10,000 acres of land as Moran State Park, on Orcas Island, Washington, citing the 1879 meeting with Muir as his inspiration.

For many Americans Muir is also an inspirational figure within the context of the American Dream; the young immigrant with very little education and no 'clout' who believed in his dream of protecting the wilderness, and who, in the land of the free, was able by hard work and belief in himself to achieve success. The ideal of American democracy offers limitless possibilities to those who want to make it from log cabin to White House, and that's what John Muir did. No wonder that he is such a hero, the farm-boy who became the confidant of Presidents, friend of the famous, recipient of honorary degrees, and one of the world's first great conservationists.

For many Americans, there's also an attendant delight in the knowledge that Muir was a 'small' man – one individual – who pitted his wits against big business, the corporations, and who won. Many of his battles were against the lumbering or mining magnates, or confronting vast farming interests. His successes remind Americans that, despite increasing corporatisation and the growth of multi-nationals, democracy provides a channel – in theory, at least – for the individual voice to be heard and for change to take place from the bottom up.

There is also the notion that, in a country where urban sprawl is a fact of life and where so many Americans find themselves distanced from the natural world, incarcerated in central-heating or air-conditioning, there is an increased need for a hero who lived the kind of life they really want – out there in the wilderness, not inside with the latest technology and the take-over bid. Muir lived the life they hanker for, he's their kind of man – and they'd be out there too if it weren't for the fact that the car needs replacing and the kitchen needs remodelling.

In the United States, Muir is often called 'the father of the National Park system', and rightly so. Under Roosevelt alone, his lobbying resulted in the creation of 148 million acres of National Forest, five National Parks and twenty three National Monuments, and after Muir's death this conservation policy continued. In 1919 the Grand Canyon (until then a National Monument) became a National Park, and in 1940 Kings Canyon National Park was formed, incorporating much of the area that Muir had originally proposed. In the year following Muir's death the Californian legislature granted the first $10,000 towards the building of the John Muir Trail from Yosemite Valley to Mount Whitney, and in 1964 the John Muir Wilderness, in east central California, was designated as one of fifty four wilderness areas.

In 1956 the John Muir Memorial Association was founded in Martinez,

> to perpetuate the memory of John Muir and his contributions to mankind, to apply his principles to the conservation of natural resources, to cause his home in Martinez to become a public shrine and to educate school children and adults in the love of nature, to preserve and protect the forests, streams and mountains of America.

In 1964 the Muir house in Martinez was designated the John Muir National Historic Site and continues to welcome visitors to the Californian mansion which for many years John and Louie Muir called home. In the same year the US Post Office issued its first Muir commemorative stamp, entitled 'John Muir, Conservationist', and a second was issued in 1998.

In Wisconsin, the John Muir Memorial Park at Fountain Lake was established in 1957, and since that date groups of students have been encouraged to visit Fountain Lake and to share in understanding the flora and fauna which Muir so loved and tried to protect. Also in Wisconsin is the Aldo Leopold Foundation and Memorial Reserve, which continues to promote the Muir ethic of appreciating and nurturing the land rather than raping it for economic gain.

The first Earth Day was celebrated on 22 April 1970; and in 1988, in recognition of the one hundred and fiftieth anniversary of Muir's birth, the United States Congress declared Muir's birthday, 21 April, 'John Muir Day'. The following year California adopted John Muir Day as an annual celebration and day of conservation, and in 1994 the Sierra Club's John Muir Exhibit website went on line, providing a feast of information on Muir. The website is updated frequently, as more work is published and more locations renamed in Muir's honour – for detailed information, see websites at the end of the bibliography.

In Canada, where Muir spent something

Delays are more and more dangerous as sundown draws nigh.

Letter to
William Trout, 1912

in the region of two years during the American Civil War, there has been less recognition of his life and achievements. The Canadian Friends of John Muir, based in Meaford, Ontario, on the shores of Georgian Bay, hold an annual John Muir Walk in June, but many Canadians remain unaware of the existence and achievements of John Muir.

In his native land of Scotland, until recent years it was very much the same picture. As the Introduction points out, given that he left Scotland at the tender age of eleven, that he achieved fame thousands of miles away, and that conservation was not a burning issue in the Scotland of his time, it's hardly surprising that Muir's name meant nothing to most of his Scottish contemporaries.

Following his death, not one of the many Muir biographies was published in Scotland. His name did not feature in the Scottish school curriculum, and with the obvious exception of friends and family, few Scots knew anything about him. As Graham White points out in his Introduction to the Scottish edition of Frederick Turner's biography of John Muir (*John Muir – From Scotland to the Sierra*), it was not until 1967, when Maimie and Bill Kimes, the Muir bibliographers, visited Dunbar, that recognition in Scotland began – slowly – to take place. At the Kimes' suggestion, a birthplace plaque was erected in 1969 at the High Street address in Dunbar. The words on the plaque reflect the somewhat sketchy local knowledge of Muir, referring to him as an 'American Naturalist', despite the fact that throughout his life he was fiercely proud of being a Scot and never regarded himself as anything else.

In 1970, on Dunbar's 600th anniversary, there was also a small Muir exhibition in the town, followed in 1976 by the opening of John Muir Country Park. The park covers 1,660 acres of the Tyne and Biel estuaries, and Belhaven Bay, and looks out towards the Bass Rock which John Muir remembered so nostalgically when he was tramping the Florida woods:

> Forgotten were the palms and magnolias and the thousand flowers that enclosed me. I could see only dulse and tangle, long-winged gulls, the Bass Rock in the Firth of Forth, and the old castle ...

*It is always
sunrise
somewhere;
the dew is
never all
dried at once;
a shower is
forever falling;
vapor is ever
rising.*

Undated journal entry

As a fitting monument to Muir, the park is not one of those tidy municipal efforts with flowers in military formation and neatly turned-out trees standing to attention. It's a nature reserve, running along the coastline for eight miles west of the old castle, with marshes and mudflats, thousands of wild seabirds and and wild sunsets. When the tide's out, you can walk for miles over the salt-glazed mud and sand, imagining the young John Muir and his first explorations into wildness:

When I was a boy in Scotland I was fond of everything that was wild, and all my life I've been growing fonder and fonder of wild places and wild things.

And it was not only in the United States that people were affected by Muir's example. Like Robert Moran, the Irish engineer whom Muir met in Alaska, individual Scots were also inspired by Muir's dream of wilderness conservation and went to considerable lengths to make his work available to a wider public. Frank Tindall of East Lothian Council was instrumental in the first small Muir exhibition in Dunbar, in the creation of John Muir Country Park, and in the eventual opening, in 1980, of the John Muir House at 128 High Street, Dunbar. Thanks to him, too, the National Library of Scotland held a Muir exhibition in 1979; and in the 1980s, concerned that most of Muir's writings remained unavailable in his native land, Tindall negotiated with Edinburgh's Canongate Publishing to bring out a number of Muir's books in Scotland.

In 1994, Dunbar's John Muir Association was formed to publicise Muir's world view and his formative years in Dunbar, and in 1999, as part of the Edinburgh International Festival, a major John Muir Exhibition, entitled An Infinite Storm of Beauty, took place to celebrate the one hundred and fiftieth anniversary of Muir's emigration from Scotland to the United States. Artefacts came from the John Muir National Historic Site in Martinez, from photographers and writers, and from the Muir family; press reports covered the exhibition, thousands of people visited; John Muir's name was heard by many Scots for the first time.

But perhaps the most valuable ongoing development in Scotland over recent years has been the creation of the John Muir Trust, founded in 1983, 'to protect and conserve wild places and to increase awareness and understanding of the value of such places'. Since 1983 the Trust has acquired six Scottish wilderness areas; 'wilderness' in Scotland refers to wild lands which, unlike wilderness areas in the United States, are homes for crofters as well as the grouse and the famed red deer. In many areas, crofters have farmed the land for generations, and there needs to be a compromise between their needs and rights, those of the flora and fauna, and the land itself.

The Trust says

> By acquiring and sensitively managing key areas of wild land, the Trust sets out to show that the damage inflicted on wild land over the centuries can be repaired. By working with the local community, the Trust aims to conserve the land on a sustainable basis for the human, animal and plant communities which share it; and that the great spiritual qualities of wildness, of tranquillity and solitude can be preserved as a legacy for those to come.

The Trust now owns three estates on the Isle of Skye: Torrin (acquired in 1991, 2,200 hectares) in the Black and Red Cuillin; Strathaird (1994, 6,500 hectares) in the heart of the Cuillin; and Sconser (1996, 3,400 hectares), a major part of the Red Cuillin Hills. On the Scottish mainland, the Li and Coire Dhorrcail estate (1987, 1,250 hectares) lies on the mountainous north coast of the Knoydart Peninsula, while Sandwood (1993, 4,650 hectares), in Sutherland, has a stunning coastline, bogland and hills. The Trust's most recent acquisition is the mystic mountain of Schiehallion, the fairy place of the Caledonians, one of the country's most-visited peaks, rising high above the shores of Loch Rannoch in the heart of Scotland.

In 1994, disturbed by the fact that 'less than a third of one per cent of (Scottish) children are actively involved in conservation',

Graham White of the City of Edinburgh Environment Centre proposed the establishment of a John Muir Award. Launched in
February 1997 and administered by the John Muir Trust, the Award
is non-competitive and open to all. Aimed primarily but not exclu-
sively at young people, and working in partnership with organisations such as the Duke of Edinburgh's Award Scheme and Venture
Scotland, it strives to involve greater numbers in the hands-on experience of conservation. The Award has three levels – Discovery/
Introductory (15 hours over 3 months), Explorer/Intermediate
(30 hours over 6 months), and Conserver/Advanced (60 hours over
12 months) – and runs a summer development programme with
participants working in peer groups in some of the wildest and most
beautiful sites in the country – Skye, Shetland, the Isle of Rum,
Arran, and many others. For contact details, see the Useful
Addresses section at the end of this Afterword.

What you can do to help, how you can get involved in conservation

John Muir entreated everyone to 'do something for wildness and
make the mountains glad'. By reading On the Trail of John Muir,
you've learned what one man did to help preserve wild places for
future generations. You can do it too. In all parts of the world,
there are local and national conservation or environmental groups
who are delighted to hear from you, and even more delighted if
you're prepared to roll up your sleeves and give practical help.
You can find them by consulting your local telephone directory,
asking your local library, or searching the web – try entering
'conservation organisations' or 'conservation groups' as key-
words, adding the name of the country or the area in which you're
interested.

Or you may want to contact one of the national or international organisations listed in the Useful Addresses section. These
are the best-known ones:

Greenpeace: a high-profile global group, whom most people associate with *Rainbow Warrior* and whose confrontational methods
often attract considerable publicity. Greenpeace describes itself as

an independent campaigning organisation which uses non-violent, creative confrontation to expose global environmental problems, and to
force the solutions which are essential to a green and peaceful future.
Greenpeace's goal is to ensure the ability of the earth to nurture life in
all its diversity.

Friends of the Earth: an international organisation founded in
1971 by four groups from France, Sweden, Britain and the United
States, campaigning at all levels on major environmental issues.
There's also a European Friends of the Earth, campaigning in 29
countries to raise public awareness and participation, and
involved in projects ranging from sustainable tourism to global
warming.

The Nature Conservancy, based in Washington DC, aims to
preserve habitats and species by buying and managing the lands
and waters these need to survive. Founded over 45 years ago, it
has more than 1,500 preserves in the United States, plus sites in
Latin America, the Caribbean and the Pacific.

In Scotland, one obvious way to get involved is via the John
Muir Trust, either as a benefactor, a volunteer, or though the John
Muir Award. On the Knoydart peninsula, volunteers have assisted
in replanting large areas of native trees and in the maintenance of
stalker's paths. On the Sandwood estate in Sutherland, collabora-
tion between the Trust and local crofting communities has resulted
in the development of sustainable tourism, with volunteers working
on footpaths and carparks which don't intrude on the beauty and
wildness of Sandwood Bay. On Strathaird, the Trust's largest
estate on the Isle of Skye, imported trees are gradually being
replaced by native species, and at Torrin, also on Skye, volunteers
have reconstructed footpaths, rebuilt drystane dykes, and established a tree nursery.

Each summer the John Muir Award scheme, in conjunction
with organisations such as the Royal Society for the Protection of
Birds and Scottish Natural Heritage, runs residential programmes
in wilderness areas. For these they need group leaders. The Award
offers one, two or six day leadership training courses in venues
such as Rum, Knoydart, Orkney, North Wales, the Lake District,

the Scottish Borders and Perthshire. If you have leadership skills, why not consider joining them?

In Muir's hometown, Dunbar's John Muir Association, founded in 1994, has established a John Muir town trail, organised a variety of Muir-related events, published a booklet on John Muir's Dunbar, and is always delighted to accept new members. If or when funding becomes available, the DJMA hopes to establish a John Muir Centre in Dunbar. In the meantime it's a partner in the John Muir Birthplace Trust, which plans to transform John Muir's birthplace into an interpretative centre on Muir's life and conservation work – again, when funds permit.

In the United States, there's the Sierra Club, whose mission statement reads

> To explore, enjoy and protect the wild places of the earth; to practise and promote the responsible use of the earth's ecosystems and resources; to educate and enlist humanity to protect and restore the quality of the natural and human environments.

They mobilise opposition to anti-conservation measures and have an extensive programme of outings and activities throughout North America – walking and mountaineering, botanising and environmental fact-finding. Whatever your perspective on the whole issue of conservation and the environment, you're likely to find something in the Sierra Club with which you want to become involved.

The National Park System of the United States consists of 378 areas covering more than 83 million acres. Commencing with the establishment of Yellowstone National Park in 1872, and considerably extended under John Muir's influence during Teddy Roosevelt's presidency, the National Park System is now part of the Federal Land Management Agencies, which also include the Bureau of Land Management (270.0 million acres), the US Forest Service (191.0 million acres), and the Fish and Wildlife Service (91.0 million acres).

Park sizes vary enormously. The largest is Wrangell-St Elias National Park and Preserve in Alaska (13,200,000 acres), and the smallest is Thaddeus Kosciuszko National Memorial in

Pennsylvania (0.02 of an acre), but regardless of size the National Parks are always happy to hear from prospective volunteers, who can find themselves liaising with park visitors or working along-side rangers high in the mountains or on the desert floor. Volunteers are particularly welcome during the summer months, when the flow of visitors is greatest, and each year the parks take on thousands of volunteer workers.

You can work in Muir's beloved High Sierra, in the summer bustle of Yosemite Valley or below the snow-capped Cathedral Range at Tuolumne Meadows. Or you can offer your help to the John Muir National Historic Site in Martinez, which is currently appealing for funds to build a new visitor centre on the site.

If you care about wild areas, as John Muir did, then you need to do something to preserve them. It's not enough to believe that others will do so, that wild areas will stay wild, that the little one individual can accomplish is just a drop in the ocean. John Muir started out with minimal education, no money and no influence, but he didn't let that deter him. He made a difference, and so can you. If you do nothing, in time, you – and your children and grandchildren – will wake up to find that there is very little wilderness left, that it has been sacrificed to the great god of economic progress. In Scotland, following devolution, there are already commercial inroads being made on the proposed National Parks. In England, walkers' right-to-roam is constantly being tested. In the United States, the Sierra Club is battling against urban sprawl and the discharge of agricultural and industrial waste into water sources. Follow John Muir's example. Get out there on the trail and make a difference.

Useful Addresses

International

Greenpeace International
Keizergracht 176
1016 DW Amsterdam
The Netherlands
Tel: 31 20 523 62 22

Friends of the Earth International
P O Box 19199
1000 GD Amsterdam
The Netherlands
Tel: 31 20 622 13 69

The Nature Conservancy - International Headquarters
4245 North Fairfax Drive, Suite 100
Arlington
VA 22203-1606
Tel: 703 841 5300

Scotland

The John Muir Trust
41 Commercial Street
Leith
Edinburgh EH6 6JD
Tel: 0131 554 0114

The John Muir Award
41 Commercial Street
Leith
Edinburgh EH6 6JD
Tel & Fax: 0131 624 7220

John Muir Birthplace Trust
128 High Street
Dunbar
East Lothian
EH42 1JJ
Tel: 01368 864329

United States

Sierra Club
85 Second Street
San Francisco
CA 94105-3441
Tel: 415 977 5500

John Muir National Historic Site
4202 Alhambra Avenue
Martinez
CA 94553-3883
Tel: 925 228 8860

Bibliography

Books by John Muir:

The Mountains of California (1894)
Our National Parks (1901)
Stickeen (1909)
Edward Henry Harriman (1911)
My First Summer in the Sierra (1911)
The Yosemite (1912)
The Story of My Boyhood and Youth (1913)
Letters to a Friend (1915)
Travels in Alaska (1915)
A Thousand Mile Walk to the Gulf (1916)
The Cruise of the Corwin (1917)
Steep Trails (1918)
John o' the Mountains: The Unpublished Journals of John Muir (1938)
Studies in the Sierra (1950)

John Muir Collections:

To the Yosemite and Beyond
(University of Wisconsin Press, Madison, 1980)

Wilderness Essays
(Peregrine Smith Books/Gibbs-Smith, Salt Lake City, 1980)

John Muir: The Eight Wilderness Discovery Books
(The Mountaineers, Seattle, and Diadem, London, 1992)

John Muir: His Life and Letters and Other Writings
(Edited by Terry Gifford) (The Mountaineers, Seattle, and Baton Wicks, London, 1996)

ADAMS, ANSEL:	*America's Wilderness: The Photographs of Ansel Adams with Writings by John Muir* (Courage Books, Philadelphia PA, 1997)
ARNOT, PHIL:	*High Sierra: John Muir's Range of Light* (Wide World-Tetra, San Carlos CA, 1996)
AUSTIN, RICHARD C.:	*Baptized into Wilderness: A Christian Perspective on John Muir* (John Knox Press, Atlanta, 1987)
BADÈ, WILLIAM F.:	*The Life and Letters of John Muir* (Houghton Mifflin, Boston, 1924)
BROWNE, E., MCQUEEN, M., EPSTEIN, A. (eds):	*The Complete Guide to America's National Parks* (Fodor's, New York, 1998)
BROWNING, PETER:	*John Muir, in His Own Words: A Book of Quotations* (Great West Books, Lafayette CA, 1998)
CLARK, LEW AND CLARK, GINNY:	*John Muir Trail Country* (Western Trails, San Luis Obispo California, 1992)
CLARKE, JAMES M.:	*The Life and Adventures of John Muir* (Sierra Club Books, San Francisco, 1980)
COHEN, MICHAEL P.:	*The Pathless Way: John Muir and American Wilderness* (University of Wisconsin Press, Madison, 1984)
EMMANUELS, GEORGE:	*John Muir, Inventor* (Panorama West Books, Fresno CA, 1984)
ENGBERG, ROBERT:	*John Muir Summering in the Sierra* (University of Wisconsin Press, Madison, 1984)
FLADER, SUSAN L. AND CALLICOT, BAIRD JO (eds):	*The River of the Mother of God and Other Essays by Aldo Leopold* (University of Wisconsin Press, Madison, 1991)

FOX, STEPHEN R.: *The American Conservation Movement: John Muir and His Legacy* (University of Wisconsin Press, Madison, 1985)

GARRETT, LEROY: *The Stone-Campbell Movement: The Story of the American Restoration Movement* (College Press Publishing, Joplin Missouri, 1981)

GIFFORD, TERRY (ed): *John Muir, His Life and Letters and Other Writings* (Mountaineers Books Seattle, and Baton Wicks, London, 1996)

GRAVES, CHARLES P.: *John Muir* (Thomas Y. Crowell, New York, 1973)

GUNSKY, FREDRIC: *South of Yosemite: Selected Writings of John Muir* (Wilderness Press, Berkeley CA, 1988)

JOHNSON, ROBERT UNDERWOOD:
Remembered Yesterdays (Little Brown, Boston, 1923)

JONES, HOLWAY: *John Muir and the Sierra Club* (Sierra Club Books, San Francisco, 1965)

KIMES, WILLIAM F. AND MAYMIE B.:
John Muir: A Reading Bibliography (Panorama West Books, Fresno CA, 1986)

LEOPOLD, ALDO: *Aldo Leopold's Wilderness: Selected Early Writings by the Author of A Sand County Almanac* (Stackpole Books, Harrisburgh PA, 1990)

LEOPOLD, ALDO: *A Sand County Almanac: And Sketches Here and There* (Oxford University Press, Oxford and New York, 1987)

LEOPOLD, LUNA B. (ED): *Round River: From the Journals of Aldo Leopold* (Oxford University Press, Oxford and New York, 1993)

LIMBAUGH, RONALD H. AND LEWIS, K.E.:
John Muir Papers, 1858-1957: Guide and Index to the Microfilm (Chadwyck-Healey, Alexandria VA, 1986)

LIMBAUGH, RONALD H.: John Muir's 'Stickeen' and the Lessons of Nature (University of Alaska Press, Fairbanks AK, 1996)

LYON, THOMAS J.: John Muir (Boise Idaho State University Western Writers Series, Boise ID, 1972)

MELHAM, TOM, AND GREHAN, FARRELL:
John Muir's Wild America (National Geographic Society, Washington DC, 1976)

MILLER, SALLY M.(ed): John Muir: Life and Work (University of New Mexico Press, Albuquerque NM, 1995)

NATIONAL PARK SERVICE:
Yosemite: Official National Park Handbook (NPS Division of Publications, US Dept of the Interior, Washington DC, 1990)

O'GRADY, JOHN P.: Pilgrims to the Wild, Everett Ruess, Henry David Thoreau, John Muir, Clarence King, Mary Austin (University of Utah Press, Salt Lake City, 1993)

PACIFIC HISTORIAN STAFF (eds):
John Muir: Life and Legacy (Holt Atherton, Stockton CA, 1986)

RUBISSOW, ARIEL AND PRIEHS, T. J. (eds):
John Muir National Historic Site (South West Parks & Monuments Association, Tucson, 1990)

SANBORN, MARGARET: Yosemite: Its Discovery, Its Wonders, and Its People (Yosemite Association/Yosemite National Park, CA, 1989)

SARGENT, SHIRLEY: *Dear Papa:Letters between John Muir and His Daughter Wanda* (Panorama Books, Fresno CA, 1985)

SARGENT, SHIRLEY: *John Muir in Yosemite* (Flying Spur, Yosemite, 1971)

SARGENT, SHIRLEY AND BROWNING, PETER:
                           Solomons of the Sierras:The Pioneer of the John Muir Trail (Flying Spur Press, Yosemite CA, 1990)

STANLEY, MILLIE: *The Heart of John Muir's World: Wisconsin, Family and Wilderness Discovery* (Prairie Oak Press, Madison WN, 1995)

STARR. WALTER A. JR: *Starr's Guide to the John Muir Trail and the High Sierra Region* (Sierra Club Books, San Francisco, 1976)

SWIFT, HILDEGARDE HOYT:
                           From the Eagle's Wings: A Biography of John Muir (William Morrow, New York, 1962)

TEALE, EDWIN W.(ed):   *The Wilderness World of John Muir* (Peter Smith, Magnolia MA, 1996)

TILTON, BUCK: *America's Wilderness: The Complete Guide to More Than 600 National Wilderness Areas* (Foghorn Press, San Francisco, 1996)

TROUT, W. H.:   *Trout Family History* (Trout, Milwaukee, 1916)

TURNER, FREDERICK: *Rediscovering America: John Muir in His Time and Ours* (Viking Penguin, New York, 1985)

VICKERY, JIM DALE: *Wilderness Visionaries: Leopold, Thoreau, Muir, Olson, Murie, Service, Marshall, Rutstrum* (Northwood Press, Minocqua WI, 1994)

WEBSTER, PAUL: *The Mighty Sierra: Portrait of a Mountain World* (American West Publishing, Palo Alto CA, 1972)

WHITE GRAHAM (ed): *Sacred Summits: John Muir's Greatest Climbs* (Canongate Books, Edinburgh, 1996)

WHITE GRAHAM (ed): *John Muir: The Wilderness Journeys* (Canongate Books, Edinburgh, 1996)

WILKINS, THURMAN: *John Muir: Apostle of Nature* (University of Oklahoma Press, Norman OK, 1995)

WINNETT, THOMAS AND MOREY, KATHY: *Guide to the John Muir Trail* (Wilderness Press, Berkeley CA, 1998)

WOLFE, LINNIE MARSH: Son of the Wilderness: The Life of John Muir (University of Wisconsin Press, Madison, 1978)

WOLFE, LINNIE MARSH (ed): John o' the Mountains: Unpublished Journals (University of Wisconsin Press, Madison, 1979)

YOUNG, SAMUEL H.: *Alaska Days with John Muir* (Ayer Company, Salem New Hampshire, 1981, reproduction of 1915 edition)

Children's books:

ANDERSON, PETER: *John Muir: Wilderness Prophet* (Franklin Watts/Grolier Publishing, New York, 1996)

DOUGLAS, WILLIAM O.: *Muir of the Mountains* (Sierra Club Books for Children, San Francisco, 1994)

DUNHAM, MONTREW: *John Muir: Young Naturalist* (Simon & Schuster Childrens, New York, 1988)

FORCE, EDEN E.:   *John Muir* (Silver Burdett Press, New
                      York, 1990)
GREENE, CAROL: *John Muir: Man of the Wild Places*
                      (Children's Press, Danbury CT, 1991)
ITO, TOM: *John Muir* (Lucent Books, San Diego
                      CA, 1996)
NADEN, CORINNE J.:   *John Muir: Saving the Wilderness*
                      (Houghton Mifflin, Boston, 1992)
TALMADGE, KATHERINE S.:
                      John Muir: At Home in the Wilderness
                      (Twenty-First Century Books, New
                      York, 1995)
TOLAN, SALLY: *John Muir* (Morehouse Publishing,
                      Harrisburgh PA, 1990)
WADSWORTH, GINGER: *John Muir: Wilderness Protector* (Lerner
                      Publishing, Minneapolis MN, 1992)

Articles:

ANDERSON, MELVILLE: 'The Conversation of John Muir', in
                      American Museum Journal, March 1915
ARDEN, HARVEY: 'John Muir's Wild America', in *National
                      Geographic*, April 1973
BROCK, MARY JANE: 'Sierra Prelude: Muir and Le Conte in
                      the South', in *Sierra Club Bulletin*,
                      March 1976
DOWNING, KEVIN J.:   'John Muir: Saving Yosemite', in
                      Scholastic Update, Vol. 126, No. 13,
                      p.15, 15 April 1994
GILLIS, MICHAEL J.:   'John Muir and the Bidwells: The
                      Forgotten Friendship', in *Dogtown
                      Territoral Quarterly*, Spring 1995
HEBERT, SANDRA: 'Wild at Heart: Nature and John Muir',
                      in *Cascade Crest* (Newsletter of the
                      Sierra Club Cascade Chapter), May/
                      June 1991
HEIDIG, EDWARD G.:   'Reflecting the Muir Image', in *Parks

and Recreation Vol. 29, No. 3 p.40,
3 March 1994

HOLMES, STEVE: 'Blessed Home: Nature, Religion, Science and Human Relationship in the Early Life of John Muir', doctoral dissertation 6/96 – see *American Quarterly* Vol. 48, Issue 4 p.761

HUBER, J. PARKER: 'John Muir's Menu', in *Sierra* Vol 79 Issue 6 p.66, November/December 1994

JOHNSON,
ROBERT UNDERWOOD: 'John Muir As I Knew Him', in *Sierra Club Bulletin*, January 1916

JOHNSON,
ROBERT UNDERWOOD: 'Personal Reminiscences of John Muir', in *Outlook*, June 3, 1905

LESHUK, DAVE: 'John Muir's Wisconsin Days: The Naturalist's Wisconsin roots anchored his later actions', in *Wisconsin Natural Resources* Vol. 12 No. 3, May/June 1988

LIMBAUGH, RONALD H.: 'John Muir and Modern Environmental Education', in *California History* Vol. 71 No. 2, Summer 1992

LIMBAUGH, RONALD H.: 'John Muir and the Mining Industry', in *Mining History Journal* No. 3 p.61-66, 1996

MARTIN, MICHELLE: 'Who Was John Muir?', in *Hi Sierran* (Newsletter of the Sierra Club San Diego Chapter), April 1991

MCKIBBIN, BILL: 'The Walk That Changed America', in *Conde Nast Traveler* Vol. 30 No.9 p.132

MERRIAM, C. HART: 'To the Memory of John Muir', in *Sierra Club Bulletin*, January 1917

MEYER, JOHN M.: 'Gifford Pinchot, John Muir, and the Boundaries of Politics in American Thought', in *Polity* Vol. 30 No.2 p.267, Winter 1997

ORSI, RICHARD: 'Wilderness Saint and Robber Baron:

The Anomalous Partnership of John Muir and the Southern Pacific Company for the Preservation of Yosemite National Park', in *Pacific Historian* Vol. 29 (2-3) pp.135-156, 1985

PARSHALL, GERALD: 'A Knight in the Wilderness: Sierra Club founder John Muir launched a movement a century ago', in *US News and World Report*, 20 July 1992

PATRICK, MARIBETH: 'A Visit with John Muir', in *Sierra Club Bulletin*, September/October 1982

PETERSON, ROBERT: 'John Muir, Protector of the Wilderness', in *Boy's Life* Vol. 84 p.28, 1 February 1994)

POLOS, NICHOLAS: 'The Educational Philosophy of John Swett and John Muir', in *Pacific Historian*, Spring 1982

SCOTT, PHYLLIS: 'John Muir National Historic Site', in *Travel Holiday* Vol. 179 Issue 4 p.17, May 1996

SMITH, MICHAEL B: 'The value of a tree: public debates of John Muir and Gifford Pinchot', in *The Historian* Vol. 60 No. 4 p.757, 22 June 1998

SMITH, MICHAEL L.: 'Clarence King and John Muir: Ways of Seeing Mountains', in *The Californians*, March/April 1990 p.36

SOLOMONS, THEODORE S.: 'The Muir of the '90s', in *The Californians*, March/April 1990 p.42

STANLEY, MILLIE: 'John Muir as Remembered by One Who Knew Him', in *Portage Daily Reporter*, July 15, 1972

STANLEY, MILLIE: 'John Muir in Wisconsin', in *Pacific Historian* Vol. 29 (2-3): 7-15, 1985

STEINHART, PETER: 'Place as purpose: Muir's Sierra', in

	Orion, Autumn 1988
SWEET, ADOLPH D.:	'Meeting John Muir in King's Canyon', in *Los Tulares* (Tulare County Historical Bulletin), September 1952
TAM, DAVID:	'John Muir for our time', in *Yodeler* (Newsletter of Sierra Club San Francisco Bay Chapter), April 1988
WILLIAMS, DENNIS:	'John Muir and an Evangelical Vision for Western Natural Resources Management', in *Journal of the West* Vol. 35 Issue 3 p.53, July 1996
WILSON, JAMES:	'John Muir: The Father of Conservation', in *The Highlander - The Magazine of Scottish Heritage* Vol. 26 No. 2, March/April 1988)
WOOD, HAROLD:	'Pantheist Prophets: John Muir 1838-1914', in *Pantheist Vision* Vol. 9 No. 2, April 1988

Supplementary Materials:

Butler, Jim, and the Environmental Interpretation Class of 1999, University of Alberta: 'The John Muir Nature Center: An Interpretive Proposal and Prospectus, Meaford, Ontario'

Periodicals devoted to John Muir:

The View From John Muir's Window, the newsletter of the John Muir Memorial Association, PO Box 2433, Martinez, CA 94553

John Muir Newsletter, John Muir Center for Regional Studies, University of the Pacific, 3601 Pacific Avenue, Stockton, CA 9521

Websites:

There are well over one million websites which include references to or information on John Muir. Some of them are of debatable quality and usefulness. The following are excellent.

www.sierraclub.org

– the Sierra Club website, containing comprehensive information on many aspects of conservation and wilderness. Here you can access details of John Muir's life and writings, the activities of the Sierra Club, the John Muir Newsletter issued by the John Muir Center for Regional Studies at the University of the Pacific, the John Muir Memorial Association, the John Muir National Historic Site at Martinez in California, details of the John Muir Youth Award, and links to a host of related sites such as the National Park Service of the United States and the John Muir Trust in Scotland.

This is also the place to find the John Muir Exhibit, compiled by Harvey Chinn and Harold Wood, and sponsored by the Sierra Club John Muir Education Project. The Exhibit is a mine of information on every aspect of Muir's life, work, beliefs, contacts, places and people with whom he was connected, and also has numerous links to related topics and sites. One of the easiest ways to use it is to access the index, which provides a complete cross-referenced list of all the subjects covered, from Alaska to Yosemite. There are on-line copies of a number of Muir's works, articles and reviews, bibliographies, John Muir associations in several countries, chronologies and genealogies, and for those 'on the trail of John Muir' there's even a section entitled Places Important to John Muir. A superb website and definitely the place to look for anything and everything connected with Muir.

www.muir-birthplace.org

– here you can access information and visuals on the town of Dunbar, where Muir was born, and take a guided tour around the Dunbar locations with which he was associated

www.johnmuir.wytbear.com

– this is the website of the Haines Alaska John Muir Association, concentrating on Muir's connections with Haines, Alaska, and the Chilkat Valley

www.nps.gov

– the website of the USA's National Park Service, with links to the individual park sites such as Yosemite and the Grand Canyon

www.jmt.org

– the site of the John Muir Trust, formed in 1983, creators of the John Muir Award and owners of a number of wild and beautiful areas in the Scottish Highlands and Islands

www.johnmuir.org

– this is the site of the Canadian Friends of John Muir, supplying information on Muir's Canadian sojourn in Trout Hollow and Meaford, Ontario

www.pantheist.net

– comprehensive information on pantheism from the Universal Pantheist Society, making available a number of essays which discuss whether or not John Muir could be considered a pantheist

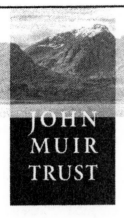

FOUNDED 1892

In 1892, John Muir, together with others concerned about the fate of the Sierra Nevada, founded the Sierra Club. With 182 charter members, the Club set about protecting forests and wildlands — first in California, then across the whole of North America.

Today, the Sierra Club has become America's oldest and largest grass-roots environmental organization. Our membership has grown, but our mission remains the same. The 65 chapters and 550,000 members of the Sierra Club are still working to explore, enjoy, protect and pre-serve our special wild places.

One thing that has changed is the composition of the organization. What was once a "club" has become a diverse democracy. Today's Sierra Club puts a strong emphasis on grassroots organizing. By informing and empowering those who care about our planet, we hope to not only improve the health of our natural world, but also to raise new generations of activists.

As John Muir famously phrased it, "When we try to pick out anything by itself, we find it hitched to everything else in the Universe." And so the Sierra Club has become active on environmental issues that cross the boundaries of state and nation. Global warming and suburban sprawl, toxic pollution and human rights — the issues have changed, but the importance of protecting our environment has not dimin-ished. After more than a century, the spirit of the Club still resonates with Muir's desire to "do something for wilderness and make the mountains glad."

For more information about the Sierra Club and its programs, please contact us using the information provided below or visit our homepage on the World Wide Web at www.sierraclub.org.

Sierra Club, 85 Second Street, Second Floor
San Francisco, CA, USA 94105-3441
TEL: (415) 977-5653 FAX: (415) 977-5799
www.sierraclub.org

THE
JOHN MUIR
BIRTHPLACE
APPEAL

The John Muir Birthplace Trust has been formed by Dunbar's John Muir Association, Dunbar Community Council, East Lothian Council and the John Muir Trust to purchase John Muir's birthplace and transform it into an interpretative centre on John Muir's life and work – and the importance of his work to the world today.

Further information about the John Muir Birthplace Trust can be found on our website at:
http://www.muir-birthplace.org

Birthplace Appeal
John Muir Birthplace Trust
128 High Street
Dunbar
East Lothian
EH42 1JJ
Scotland

DUNBAR'S JOHN MUIR ASSOCIATION

DJMA is committed to a policy of sustainability. Underlying all the Association's activities will be the guiding principles of

- using resources wisely;

- living within the carrying capacity of the environment;

- promoting environmental quality;

- adopting the precautionary principle;

- accepting our environmental responsibilities.

Wherever you live, you can help to realise these goals by joining Dunbar's John Muir Association and giving it your support. To obtain a membership application form, please contact

Mr Jim Thompson
Subscription Secretary
DJMA
43 Beachmont Place
Dunbar
East Lothian
EH42 1YE
Scotland

Tel: 01368 863162

Index

Africa 91

Agassiz, Louis 27, 57

Alaska 66,83

Alaska Days with John Muir 67

Alaska, Harriman Expedition
  to 82

Alhambra 64,71

Amazon 92

American Civil War 10,28

anthropocentrism 44

Arizona 81,88

Athens, Georgia 48

Atlantic Monthly 82

Back Street Café 36

Badè, Frederic William
  21,36,43,62,97

Bamburgh Close, Dunbar 6

baobab trees 92

Bass Rock 49,100

Battle of Bannockburn 11

Bering Sea 83

Bering Strait 76

Big Head River 39

Billy the Shepherd 55

Black Agnes 11

black bears xxi

blinding, of John Muir 41

Blue Forest 88

Blue Mesa 88

Bonaventure 47,48

Boston Recorder 31

Bresnahan, Connie 39

Bridalveil Meadow 84

Bright Angel Trail 86,87

Brownie 61

Bruce, Robert the 9,11

Burcher, Robert 39

Burns, Robert xviii,1,42

Butler, Dr James Davie 27,31,56

Burroughs, John 83

Californian Gold Rush 13

Calypso Borealis 31

Camp Randall 28,30

Canadian Friends of John Muir,
  The 38,100

Canadians 32

Canby, William 82

Carr, Ezra Slocum 26,57,62

Carr, Jeanne 26,27,41,61,93

Cedar Keys 49

Century, The 78,81

Chilcat Indians 66

Chilean Andes 92

Chillwell, Joseph 51,52,53

choke-damp, effects of 23

Christianity xxiii

Clark, Galen 73

Cleveland, President 81

Coulterville, California 52

Cross Sound, Alaska 74

Some other books published by **LUATH** PRESS

ON THE TRAIL OF

On the Trail of Robert Service

GW Lockhart

ISBN 0 946487 24 3 PBK £7.99

 Robert Service is famed world-wide for his eye-witness verse-pictures of the Klondike goldrush. As a war poet, his work outsold Owen and Sassoon, and he went on to become the world's first million selling poet. In search of adventure and new experiences, he emigrated from Scotland to Canada in 1890 where he was caught up in the aftermath of the raging gold fever. His vivid dramatic verse bring to life the wild, larger than life characters of the gold rush Yukon, their bar-room brawls, their lust for gold, their trigger-happy gambles with life and love. 'The Shooting of Dan McGrew' is perhaps his most famous poem:

> A bunch of the boys were whooping it
> up in the Malamute saloon;
> The kid that handles the music box
> was hitting a ragtime tune;
> Back of the bar in a solo game, sat
> Dangerous Dan McGrew,
> And watching his luck was his light
> o'love, the lady that's known as Lou.

His storytelling powers have brought Robert Service enduring fame, particularly in North America and Scotland where he is something of a cult figure. Starting in Scotland, *On the Trail of Robert Service* follows Service as he wanders through British Columbia, Oregon, California, Mexico, Cuba, Tahiti, Russia, Turkey and the Balkans, finally 'settling' in France.

This revised edition includes an expanded selection of illustrations of scenes from the Klondike as well as several photographs from the family of Robert Service on his travels around the world.

Wallace Lockhart, an expert on Scottish traditional folk music and dance, is the author of *Highland Balls & Village Halls* and *Fiddles & Folk*. His relish for a well-told tale in popular vernacular led him to fall in love with the verse of Robert Service and write his biography.

A fitting tribute to a remarkable man – a bank clerk who wanted to become a cowboy. It is hard to imagine a bank clerk writing such lines as:

A bunch of boys were whooping it up... The income from his writing actually exceeded his bank salary by a factor of five and he resigned to pursue a full time writing career.

Charles Munn, THE SCOTTISH BANKER

Robert Service claimed he wrote for those who wouldnit be seen dead reading poetry. His was an almost unbelievably mobile life... Lockhart hangs on breathlessly, enthusiastically unearthing clues to the poet's life.

Ruth Thomas, SCOTTISH BOOK COLLECTOR

This enthralling biography will delight Service lovers in both the Old World and the New.

Marilyn Wright, SCOTS INDEPENDENT

On the Trail of William Wallace

David R. Ross

ISBN 0 946487 47 2   PBK   £7.99

How close to reality was *Braveheart*?

Where was Wallace actually born?

What was the relationship between Wallace and Bruce?

Are there any surviving eye-witness accounts of Wallace?

How does Wallace influence the psyche of today's Scots?

On the Trail of William Wallace offers a refreshing insight into the life and heritage of the great Scots hero whose proud story is at the very heart of what it means to be Scottish. Not concentrating simply on the hard historical facts of Wallace's life, the book also takes into account the real significance of Wallace and his effect on the ordinary Scot through the ages, manifested in the many sites where his memory is marked.

In trying to piece together the jigsaw of the reality of Wallace's life, David Ross weaves a subtle flow of new information with his own observations. His engaging, thoughtful and at times amusing narrative reads with the ease of a historical novel, complete with all the intrigue, treachery and romance required to hold the attention of the casual reader and still entice the more knowledgable historian.

74 places to visit in Scotland and the north of England

One general map and 3 location maps

Stirling and Falkirk battle plans

Wallace's route through London

Chapter on Wallace connections in North America and elsewhere

Reproductions of rarely seen illustrations

On the Trail of William Wallace will be enjoyed by anyone with an interest in Scotland, from the passing tourist to the most fervent nationalist. It is an encyclopaedia-cum-guide book, literally stuffed with fascinating titbits not usually on offer in the conventional history book.

David Ross is organiser of and historical adviser to the Society of William Wallace.

Historians seem to think all there is to be known about Wallace has already been uncovered. Mr Ross has proved that Wallace studies are in fact in their infancy.
ELSPETH KING, Director the the Stirling Smith Art Museum & Gallery, who annotated and introduced the recent Luath edition of *Blind Harry's Wallace*.

'Better the pen than the sword!'

RANDALL WALLACE, author of *Braveheart*, when asked by David Ross how it felt to be partly responsible for the freedom of a nation following the Devolution Referendum.

On the Trail of Robert the Bruce

David R. Ross

ISBN 0 946487 52 9 PBK £7.99

On the Trail of Robert the Bruce charts the story of Scotland's hero-king from his boyhood, through his days of indecision as Scotland suffered under the English yoke, to his assumption of the crown exactly six months after the death of William Wallace. Here is the astonishing blow by blow account of how, against fearful odds, Bruce led the Scots to win their greatest ever victory. Bannockburn was not the end of the story. The war against English oppression lasted another fourteen years. Bruce lived just long enough to see his dreams of an independent Scotland come to fruition in 1328 with the signing of the Treaty of Edinburgh. The trail takes us to Bruce sites in Scotland, many of the little known and forgotten battle sites in northern England, and as far afield as the Bruce monuments in Andalusia and Jerusalem.

67 places to visit in Scotland and elsewhere.

One general map, 3 location maps and a map of Bruce-connected sites in Ireland.

Bannockburn battle plan.

Drawings and reproductions of rarely seen illustrations.

On the Trail of Robert the Bruce is not all blood and gore. It brings out the love and laughter, pain and passion of one of the great eras of Scottish history.

Read it and you will understand why David Ross has never knowingly killed a spider in his life. Once again, he proves himself a master of the popular brand of hands-on history that made *On the Trail of William Wallace* so popular.

'David R. Ross is a proud patriot and unashamed romantic.'

SCOTLAND ON SUNDAY

'Robert the Bruce knew Scotland, knew every class of her people, as no man who ruled her before or since has done. It was he who asked of her a miracle – and she accomplished it.'

AGNES MUIR MACKENZIE

On the Trail of Mary Queen of Scots

J. Keith Cheetham
ISBN 0 946487 50 2   PBK   £7.99

Life dealt Mary Queen of Scots love, intrigue, betrayal and tragedy in generous measure.

On the Trail of Mary Queen of Scots traces the major events in the turbulent life of the beautiful, enigmatic queen whose romantic reign and tragic destiny exerts an undimmed fascination over 400 years after her execution.

Places of interest to visit – 99 in Scotland, 35 in England and 29 in France.

One general map and 6 location maps.

Line drawings and illustrations.

Simplified family tree of the royal houses of Tudor and Stuart.

Key sites include:

Linlithgow Palace – Mary's birthplace, now a magnificent ruin

Stirling Castle – where, only nine months old, Mary was crowned Queen of Scotland

Notre Dame Cathedral – where, aged fifteen, she married the future king of France

The Palace of Holyroodhouse – Rizzio, one of Mary's closest advisers, was murdered here and some say his blood still stains the spot where he was stabbed to death

Sheffield Castle – where for fourteen years she languished as prisoner of her cousin, Queen Elizabeth I

Fotheringhay – here Mary finally met her death on the executioner's block.

On the Trail of Mary Queen of Scots is for everyone interested in the life of perhaps the most romantic figure in Scotland's history; a thorough guide to places connected with Mary, it is also a guide to the complexities of her personal and public life.

'In my end is my beginning'
MARY QUEEN OF SCOTS

'...the woman behaves like the Whore of Babylon'
JOHN KNOX

NATURAL SCOTLAND

Wild Scotland: The essential guide to finding the best of natural Scotland

James McCarthy
Photography by Laurie Campbell
ISBN 1 84282 096 6 PBK £8.99

With a foreword by Magnus Magnusson and striking colour photographs by Laurie Campbell, this is the essential up-to-date guide to viewing wildlife in Scotland for the visitor and resident alike. It provides a fascinating overview of the country's plants, animals, bird and marine life against the background of their typical natural settings, as an introduction to the vivid descriptions of the most accessible localities, linked to clear regional maps. A unique feature is the focus on 'green tourism' and sustainable visitor use of the countryside, contributed by Duncan Bryden, manager of the Scottish Tourist Board's Tourism and the Environment Task Force. Important practical information on access and the best times of year for viewing sites makes this an indispensable and user-friendly travelling companion to anyone interested in exploring Scotland's remarkable natural heritage.

James McCarthy is former Deputy Director for Scotland of the Nature Conservancy Council, and now a Board Member of Scottish Natural Heritage and Chairman of the Environmental Youth Work National Development Project Scotland.

'Nothing but Heather!'

Gerry Cambridge
ISBN 0 946487 49 9 PBK £15.00

Enter the world of Scottish nature – bizarre, brutal, often beautiful, always fascinating – as seen through the lens and poems of Gerry Cambridge, one of Scotland's most distinctive contemporary poets.

On film and in words, Cambridge brings unusual focus to bear on lives as diverse as those of dragonflies, hermit crabs, short-eared owls, and wood anemones. The result is both an instructive look by a naturalist at some of the flora and fauna of Scotland and a poet's aesthetic journey.

This exceptional collection comprises 48 poems matched with 48 captioned photographs. In his introduction Cambridge explores the origins of the project and the approaches to nature taken by other poets, and incorporates a wry account of an unwillingly-sectarian, farm-labouring, bird-obsessed adolescence in rural Ayrshire in the 1970s.

Keats felt that the beauty of a rainbow was somehow tarnished by knowledge of its properties. Yet the natural world is surely made more, not less, marvellous by awareness of its workings. In the poems that accompany these pictures, I have tried to give an inkling of that. May the marriage of verse and image enlarge the reader's appreciation and, perhaps, insight into the chomping, scurrying, quivering, procreating and dying kingdom, however many miles it be beyond the door.
GERRY CAMBRIDGE

a real poet, with a sense of the music of language and the poetry of life...
KATHLEEN RAINE

one of the most promising and original of modern Scottish poets... a master of form and subtlety.
GEORGE MACKAY BROWN

Scotland Land and People
An Inhabited Solitude

James McCarthy

ISBN 0 946487 57 X PBK £7.99

Scotland is the country above all others that I have seen, in which a man of imagination may carve out his own pleasures; there are so many inhabited solitudes.

DOROTHY WORDSWORTH, in her journal of August 1803

An informed and thought-provoking profile of Scotland's unique landscapes and the impact of humans on what we see now and in the future. James McCarthy leads us through the many aspects of the land and the people who inhabit it: natural Scotland; the rocks beneath; land ownership; the use of resources; people and place; conserving Scotland's heritage and much more.

Written in a highly readable style, this concise volume offers an under-standing of the land as a whole. Emphasising the uniqueness of the Scottish environment, the author explores the links between this and other aspects of our culture as a key element in rediscovering a modern sense of the Scottish identity and perception of nationhood.

This book provides an engaging introduc-

tion to the mysteries of Scotland's people and landscapes. Difficult concepts are described in simple terms, providing the interested Scot or tourist with an invaluable overview of the country... It fills an important niche which, to my knowledge, is filled by no other publications.

BETSY KING, Chief Executive, Scottish Environmental Education Council.

The Highland Geology Trail

John L Roberts

ISBN 0946487 36 7 PBK £4.99

Where can you find the oldest rocks in Europe?
Where can you see ancient hills around 800 million years old?
How do you tell whether a valley was carved out by a glacier, not a river?
What are the Fucoid Beds?
Where do you find rocks folded like putty?
How did great masses of rock pile up like snow in front of a snow-plough?
When did volcanoes spew lava and ash to form Skye, Mull and Rum?
Where can you find fossils on Skye?

...a lucid introduction to the geological record in general, a jargon-free exposition of the regional background, and a series of descriptions of specific localities of geological interest on a 'trail' around the highlands.

Having checked out the local references on the ground, I can vouch for their accuracy and look forward to investigating farther afield, informed by this guide.

Great care has been taken to explain specific terms as they occur and, in so doing, John Roberts has created a resource of great value which is eminently usable by anyone with an interest in the outdoors...the best bargain you are likely to get as a geology book in the foreseeable future.

Jim Johnston, PRESS AND JOURNAL

Rum: Nature's Island

Magnus Magnusson

ISBN 0 946487 32 4   £7.95 PBK

Rum: Nature's Island is the fascinating story of a Hebridean island from the earliest times through to the Clearances and its period as the sporting playground of a Lancashire industrial magnate, and on to its rebirth as a National Nature Reserve, a model for the active ecological management of Scotland's wild places.

Thoroughly researched and written in a lively accessible style, the book includes comprehensive coverage of the island's geology, animals and plants, and people, with a special chapter on the Edwardian extravaganza of Kinloch Castle. There is practical information for visitors to what was once known as 'the Forbidden Isle'; the book provides details of bothy and other accommodation, walks and nature trails. It closes with a positive vision for the island's future: biologically diverse, economically dynamic and ecologically sustainable.

Rum: Nature's Island is published in co-operation with Scottish Natural Heritage (of which Magnus Magnusson is Chairman) to mark the 40th anniversary of the acquisition of Rum by its predecessor, The Nature Conservancy.

Red Sky at Night

John Barrington

ISBN 0 946487 60 X   £8.99

I read John Barrington's book with growing delight. This working shepherd writes beautifully about his animals, about the wildlife, trees and flowers which surround him at all times, and he paints an unforgettable picture of his glorious corner of Western Scotland. It is a lovely story of a rather wonderful life.

JAMES HERRIOT

John Barrington is a shepherd to over 750 Blackface ewes who graze 2,000 acres of some of Britain's most beautiful hills overlooking the deep dark water of Loch Katrine in Perthshire. The yearly round of lambing, dipping, shearing and the sales is marvellously interwoven into the story of the glen, of Rob Roy in whose house John now lives, of curling when the ice is thick enough, and of sheep dog trials in the summer. Whether up to the hills or along the glen, John knows the haunts of the local wildlife: the wily hill fox, the grunting badger, the herds of red deer, and the shrews, voles and insects which scurry underfoot. He sets his seasonal clock by the passage of birds on the loch, and jealously guards over the golden eagle's eyrie in the hills. Paul Armstrong's sensitive illustrations are the perfect accompaniment to the evocative text.

Mr Barrington is a great pleasure to read. One learns more things about the countryside from this account of one year than from a decade of The Archers.

THE DAILY TELEGRAPH

Powerful and evocative... a book which brings vividly to life the landscape, the wildlife, the farm animals and the people who inhabit John's vista. He makes it easy for the reader to fall in love with both his surrounds and his commune with nature.

THE SCOTTISH FIELD

An excellent and informative book.... not only an account of a shepherd's year but also the diary of a naturalist. Little escapes Barrington's enquiring eye and, besides the life cycle of a sheep, he also gives those of every bird, beast, insect and plant that crosses his path, mixing their histories with descriptions of the geography, local history and folklore of his surroundings.

TLS

The family life at Glengyle is wholesome, appealing and not without a touch of the Good Life. Many will envy Mr Barrington his fastness home as they cruise up Loch Katrine on the tourist steamer.

THE FIELD

Listen to the Trees

Don MacCaskill

ISBN 0 946487 65 0   £9.99 PBK

Don MacCaskill is one of Scotland's foremost naturalists, conservationists and wildlife photographers. *Listen to the Trees is a beautiful and acutely observed account of* how his outlook on life began to change as trees, woods, forests and all the wonders that they contain became a focus in his life. It is rich in its portrayal of the life that moves in the Caledonian forest and on the moorlands – lofty twig-stacked heronries, the elusive peregrine falcon and the red, bushy-tailed fox – of the beauty of the trees, and of those who worked in the forests.

'Trees are surely the supreme example of a life-force stronger than our own,' writes Don MacCaskill. 'Some, like the giant redwoods of North America, live for thousands of years. Some, like our own oaks and pines, may live for centuries. All, given the right conditions, will regenerate their species and survive long into the future.'

In the afterword Dr Philip Ratcliffe, former Head of the Forestry Commission's Environment Branch and a leading environment consultant, discusses the future role of Britain's forests – their influence on the natural environment and on the communities that live and work in and around them.

Listen to the Trees will inspire all those with an interest in nature. It is a beautiful account, strongly anecdotal and filled with humour.

RENNIE MCOWAN

This man adores trees. 200 years from now, your descendants will know why.

JIM GILCHRIST, THE SCOTSMAN

LUATH GUIDES TO SCOTLAND

These guides are not your traditional where-to-stay and what-to-eat books. They are companions in the rucksack or car seat, providing the discerning traveller with a blend of fiery opinion and moving description. Here you will find *'that curious pastiche of myths and legend and history that the Scots use to describe their heritage... what battle happened in which glen between which clans; where the Picts sacrificed bulls as recently as the 17th*

century... A lively counterpoint to the more standard, detached guidebook... Intriguing.
THE WASHINGTON POST

These are perfect guides for the discerning visitor or resident to keep close by for reading again and again, written by authors who invite you to share their intimate knowledge and love of the areas covered.

Mull and Iona: Highways and Byways

Peter Macnab

ISBN 1 84282 089 3 PBK £4.99

'The Isle of Mull is of Isles the fairest,
Of ocean's gems 'tis the first and rarest.'
So a local poet described it a hundred years ago, and this recently revised guide to Mull and sacred Iona, the most accessible islands of the Inner Hebrides, takes the reader on a delightful tour of these rare ocean gems, travelling with a native whose unparalleled knowledge and deep feeling for the area unlock the byways of the islands in all their natural beauty.

South West Scotland

Tom Atkinson

ISBN 1 905222 15 7 PBK £5.99

This descriptive guide to the magical country of Robert Burns covers Kyle, Carrick, Galloway, Dumfriesshire, Kirkcudbrightshire and Wigtownshire. Hills, unknown moors and unspoiled beaches grace a land steeped in history and legend and portrayed with affection and deep delight.

An essential book for the visitor who yearns to feel at home in this land of peace and grandeur.

The West Highlands: The Lonely Lands

Tom Atkinson

ISBN 1 84282 088 5 PBK £5.99

A guide to Inveraray, Glencoe, Loch Awe, Loch Lomond, Cowal, the Kyles of Bute and all of central Argyll written with insight, sympathy and loving detail. Once Atkinson has taken you there, these lands can never feel lonely. 'I have sought to make the complex simple, the beautiful accessible and the strange familiar,' he writes, and indeed he brings to the land a knowledge and affection only accessible to someone with intimate knowledge of the area.

A must for travellers and natives who want to delve beneath the surface.

'Highly personal and somewhat quirky... steeped in the lore of Scotland.
THE WASHINGTON POST

The Northern Highlands: The Empty Lands

Tom Atkinson

ISBN 1 84282 087 7 PBK £5.99

The Highlands of Scotland from Ullapool to Bettyhill and Bonar Bridge to John O' Groats are landscapes of myth and legend, 'empty of people, but of nothing else that brings delight to any tired soul,' writes Atkinson. This highly personal guide describes Highland history and landscape with love, compassion and above all sheer magic.

Essential reading for anyone who has dreamed of the Highlands.

The North West Highlands: Roads to the Isles

Tom Atkinson

ISBN 1 84282 086 9 PBK £5.99

Ardnamurchan, Morvern, Morar, Moidart and the west coast to Ullapool are included in this guide to the Far West and Far North of Scotland. An unspoiled land of mountains, lochs and silver sands is brought to the walker's toe-tips (and to the reader's fingertips) in this stark, serene and evocative account of town, country and legend.

For any visitor to this Highland wonderland, Queen Victoria's favourite place on earth.

WALK WITH LUATH

Mountain Days & Bothy Nights

Dave Brown and Ian Mitchell

ISBN 0 946487 15 4 PBK £7.50

Acknowledged as a classic of mountain writing still in demand ten years after its first publication, this book takes you into the bothies, howffs and dosses on the Scottish hills. Fishgut Mac, Desperate Dan and Stumpy the Big Yin stalk hill and public house, evading gamekeepers and Roy-

alty with a camaraderie which was the trademark of Scots hillwalking in the early days.

'The fun element comes through... how innocent the social polemic seems in our nastier world of today... the book for the rucksack this year.*

Hamish Brown,
SCOTTISH MOUNTAINEERING CLUB JOURNAL

The Joy of Hillwalking

Ralph Storer

ISBN 0 946487 28 6 PBK £7.50

Apart, perhaps, from the joy of sex, the joy of hillwalking brings more pleasure to more people than any other form of human activity.

Alps, America, Scandinavia, you name it – Storer's been there, so why the hell shouldn't he bring all these various and varied places into his observations... [He] even admits to losing his virginity after a day on the Aggy Ridge... Well worth its place alongside Storer's earlier works. TAC

Scotland's Mountains before the Mountaineers

Ian Mitchell

ISBN 0 946487 39 1 PBK £9.99

In this ground-breaking book, Ian Mitchell tells the story of explorations and ascents in the Scottish Highlands in the days before mountaineering became a popular sport – when bandits, Jacobites, poachers and illicit distillers traditionally used the mountains as sanctuary. The book also gives a detailed account of the map makers, road builders, geologists, astronomers and naturalists, many of whom ascended hitherto untrodden summits while working in the Scottish Highlands.

Scotland's Mountains before the Mountaineers is divided into four Highland regions, with a map of each region showing key summits. While not designed primarily as a guide, it will be a useful handbook for walkers and climbers. Based on a wealth of new research, this book offers a fresh perspective that will fascinate climbers and mountaineers and everyone interested in the history of mountaineering, cartography, the evolution of landscape and the social history of the Scottish Highlands.

LUATH WALKING GUIDES

The highly respected and continually updated guides to the Cairngorms.

'Particularly good on local wildlife and how to see it'
THE COUNTRYMAN

Hill Walks in the Cairngorms
Ernest Cross
ISBN 1 84282 092 3 £4.99

This selection of some of the most popular hill walks in the beautiful Cairngorms makes a detailed and lively companion for hillwalkers of all ages. Cross demonstrates his knowledge, love and considerable experience of walking in the Cairngorms with this varied and rewarding guide to the hills

and to nearby Badenoch – commonly known as Monarch of the Glen country after being popularised by the BBC television series.

Including a step-by-step route plan for each walk, invaluable mountain safety tips and practical local advice, *Hill Walks in the Cairngorms* also makes inspiring reading for the armchair hillwalker by incorporating a comprehensive guide to the wildlife, history and surroundings of the area to make the Cairngorm landscape come alive.

Easy Walks in Monarch of the Glen Country: Badenoch and Strathspey
Ernest Cross
ISBN 1 84282 093 1 £4.99

Based on its predecessor, Short Walks in the Cairngorms, this book is a clear and comprehensive guide to a selection of easygoing yet scenic walks in the areas of Scottish countryside made popular by the BBC television series Monarch of the Glen. Perfect for novice and amateur walkers as well as families, *Easy Walks in Monarch of the Glen Country* is a lively pocket companion that provides a wealth of information to the reader, including detailed route plans of each walk, invaluable safety tips, basic hillwalking instruction and practical local advice.

A comprehensive guide to the wildlife, history and surroundings of the area, this book helps bring the Cairngorm landscape alive. On the hills or at home by the fire, *Easy Walks in Monarch of the Glen Country* makes inspiring reading for anyone interested in walking in the Cairngorm area.

Short Walks on Skye

Joanna Young
ISBN 1 84282 065 6 £4.99

This book describes forty short walks on Skye: the shortest is only a couple of minutes, the longest no more than 35.

Joanna Young wrote this book after family holidays in Skye revealed the need for short walks suitable for all ages, fitness levels and motivation as well as all weather conditions.

FOLKLORE
The Supernatural Highlands

Francis Thompson
ISBN 0 946487 31 6 PBK £8.99

An authoritative exploration of the other-world of the Highlander, happenings and beings hitherto thought to be outwith the ordinary forces of nature. A simple introduction to the way of life of rural Highland and Island communities, this new edition weaves a path through second sight, the evil eye, witchcraft, ghosts, fairies and other supernatural beings, offering new sight-lines on areas of belief once dismissed as folklore and superstition.

Tall Tales from an Island

Peter Macnab
ISBN 0 946487 07 3 PBK £8.99

Peter Macnab was born and reared on Mull. He heard many of these tales as a lad, and others he has listened to in later years.

There are humorous tales, grim tales,

witty tales, tales of witchcraft, tales of love, tales of heroism, tales of treachery, historical tales and tales of yesteryear.

A popular lecturer, broadcaster and writer, Peter Macnab is the author of a number of books and articles about Mull, the island he knows so intimately and loves so much. As he himself puts it in his introduction to this book 'I am of the unswerving opinion that nowhere else in the world will you find a better way of life, nor a finer people with whom to share it.'

All islands, it seems, have a rich store of characters whose stories represent a kind of sub-culture without which island life would be that much poorer. Macnab has succeeded in giving the retelling of the stories a special Mull flavour, so much so that one can visualise the storytellers sitting on a bench outside the house with a few cronies, puffing on their pipes and listening with nodding approval.
WEST HIGHLAND FREE PRESS

Tales from the North Coast

Alan Temperley
ISBN 0 946487 18 9 PBK £8.99

Seals and shipwrecks, witches and fairies, curses and clearances, fact and fantasy – the authentic tales in this collection come straight from the heart of a small Highland community. Children and adults alike responsd to their timeless appeal. These *Tales of the North Coast* were collected in the early 1970s by Alan Temperley and young people at Farr Secondary School in Sutherland. All the stories were gathered from the area between the Kyle of Tongue and Strath Halladale, in scattered communities wonderfully rich in lore that had been passed on by word of mouth down the generations. This wide-ranging selection provides a satisying balance between intriguing tales of the supernatural and more everyday occurrences. The book also includes chilling eye-witness accounts of the notorious Strathnaver Clearances when tenants were given a few hours to pack up and get out of their homes, which were then burned to the ground.

Underlying the continuity through the generations, this new edition has a foreward by Jim Johnston, the head teacher at Farr, and includes the vigorous linocut images produced by the young people under the guidance of their art teacher, Elliot Rudie.

Since the original publication of this book, Alan Temperley has gone on to become a highly regarded writer for children.

The general reader will find this book's spontaneity, its pictures by the children and its fun utterly charming.
SCOTTISH REVIEW

An admirable book which should serve as an encouragement to other districts to gather what remains of their heritage of folk-tales.
SCOTTISH EDUCATION JOURNAL

NEW SCOTLAND

Scotland – Land and Power the agenda for land reform

Andy Wightman
in association with
Democratic Left Scotland
foreword by Lesley Riddoch
ISBN 0 946487 70 7 PBK £5.00

What is land reform?
Why is it needed?
Will the Scottish Parliament really make a difference?
Scotland – Land and Power argues passionately that nothing less than a radical, comprehensive programme of land reform can make the difference that is needed. Now is no time for palliative solutions which treat the symptoms and not the causes.

Scotland – Land and Power is a controversial and provocative book that clarifies the complexities of landownership in Scotland. Andy Wightman explodes the myth that land issues are relevant only to the far flung fringes of rural Scotland, and questions mainstream political commitment to land reform. He presents his own far-reaching programme for change and a pragmatic, inspiring vision of how Scotland can move from outmoded, unjust power structures towards a more equitable landowning democracy.

'Writers like Andy Wightman are determined to make sure that the hurt of the last century is not compounded by a rushed solution in the next. This accessible, comprehensive but passionately argued book is quite simply essential reading and perfectly timed – here's hoping Scotland's legislators agree.'
LESLEY RIDDOCH

Old Scotland New Scotland

Jeff Fallow

ISBN 0 946487 40 5 PBK £6.99

Together we can build a new Scotland based on Labour's values.

DONALD DEWAR, Party Political Broad-cast

Despite the efforts of decent Mr Dewar, the voters may yet conclude they are looking at the same old hacks in brand new suits.

IAN BELL, *The Independent*

At times like this you suddenly realise how dangerous the neglect of Scottish history in our schools and universities may turn out to be.

MICHAEL FRY, *The Herald*

...one of the things I hope will go is our chip on the shoulder about the English... The SNP has a huge responsibility to articulate Scottish independence in a way that is pro-Scottish and not anti-English.

ALEX SALMOND, *The Scotsman*

Scottish politics have never been more exciting. In *old Scotland new Scotland* Jeff Fallow takes us on a graphic voyage through Scotland's turbulent history, from earliest times through to the present day and beyond. This fast-track guide is the quick way to learn what your history teacher didn't tell you, essential reading for all who seek an understanding of Scotland and its history.

Eschewing the romanticisation of his country's past, Fallow offers a new perspective on an old nation. 'Too many people associate Scottish history with tartan trivia or outworn romantic myth. This book aims to blast that stubborn idea.'

JEFF FALLOW

Notes from the North

incorporating a Brief History of the Scots and the English

Emma Wood

ISBN 0 946487 46 4 PBK £8.99

Notes on being English
Notes on being in Scotland
Learning from a shared past

Sickened by the English jingoism that surfaced in rampant form during the 1982 Falklands War, Emma Wood started to dream of moving from her home in East Anglia to the Highlands of Scotland. She felt increasingly frustrated and marginalised as Thatcherism got a grip on the southern English psyche. The Scots she met on frequent holidays in the Highlands had no truck with Thatcherism, and she felt at home with grass-roots Scottish anti-authoritarianism. The decision was made. She uprooted and headed for a new life in the north of Scotland.

An intelligent and perceptive book... calm, reflective, witty and sensitive. It should certainly be read by all English visitors to Scotland, be they tourists or incomers. And it should certainly be read by all Scots concerned about what kind of nation we live in. They might learn something about themselves.

THE HERALD

... her enlightenment is evident on every page of this perceptive, provocative book.

MAIL ON SUNDAY

FICTION
The Bannockburn Years
William Scott
ISBN 0 946487 34 0 PBK £7.95

A present day Edinburgh solicitor stumbles across reference to a document of value to the Nation State of Scotland. He tracks down the document on the Isle of Bute, a document which probes the real 'quaestiones' about nationhood and national identity. The document ends up being published, but is it authentic and does it matter? Almost 700 years on, these 'quaestiones' are still worth asking.

Written with pace and passion, William Scott has devised an intriguing vehicle to open up new ways of looking at the future of Scotland and its people. He presents an alternative interpretation of how the Battle of Bannockburn was fought, and through the Bannatyne manuscript he draws the reader into the minds of those involved.

Winner of the 1997 Constable Trophy, the premier award in Scotland for an unpublished novel, this book offers new insights to both the academic and the general reader which are sure to provoke further discussion and debate.

A brilliant storyteller. I shall expect to see your name writ large hereafter.

NIGEL TRANTER, October 1997.

... a compulsive read.

PH Scott, THE SCOTSMAN

The Great Melnikov
Hugh MacLachlan
ISBN 0 946487 42 1 PBK £7.95

A well crafted, gripping novel, written in a style reminiscent of John Buchan and set in London and the Scottish Highlands during the First World War, *The Great Melnikov* is a dark tale of double-cross and deception. We first meet Melnikov, one-time star of the German circus, languishing as a down-and-out in Trafalgar Square. He soon finds himself drawn into a tortuous web of intrigue. He is a complex man whose personal struggle with alcoholism is an inner drama which parallels the tense twists and turns as a spy mystery unfolds. Melnikov's options are narrowing. The circle of threat is closing. Will Melnikov outwit the sinister enemy spy network? Can he summon the will and the wit to survive?

Hugh MacLachlan, in his first full length novel, demonstrates an undoubted ability to tell a good story well. His earlier stories have been broadcast on Radio Scotland, and he has the rare distinction of being shortlisted for the Macallan/Scotland on Sunday Short Story Competition two years in succession.

HISTORY
Blind Harry's Wallace
William Hamilton of Gilbertfield
Introduced by Elspeth King
ISBN 0 946487 43 X HBK £15.00
ISBN 0 946487 33 2 PBK £8.99
The original story of the real braveheart, Sir William Wallace. Racy, blood on every page, violently anglo-phobic,

grossly em-bellished, vulgar and disgusting, clumsy and stilted, a literary failure, a great epic.

Whatever the verdict on blind harry, this is the book which has done more than any other to frame the notion of Scotland's national identity. Despite its numerous 'historical inaccuracies', it remains the principal source for what we now know about the life of Wallace.

The novel and film *Braveheart* were based on the 1722 Hamilton edition of this epic poem. Burns, Wordsworth, Byron and others were greatly influenced by this version 'wherein the old obsolete words are rendered more intelligible', which is said to be the book, next to the Bible, most commonly found in Scottish households in the eighteenth century. Burns even admits to having 'borrowed... a couplet worthy of Homer' directly from Hamilton's version of blind harry to include in '*Scots wha hae*'.

Elspeth King, in her introduction to this, the first accessible edition of blind harry in verse form since 1859, draws parallels between the situation in Scotland at the time of Wallace and that in Bosnia and Chechnya in the 1990s. Seven hundred years to the day after the Battle of Stirling Bridge, the 'Settled Will of the Scottish People' was expressed in the devolution referendum of 11 September 1997. She describes this as a landmark opportunity for mature reflection on how the nation has been shaped, and sees blind harry's wallace as an essential and compelling text for this purpose.

A true bard of the people.

TOM SCOTT, THE PENGUIN BOOK OF SCOTTISH VERSE, on Blind Harry.

A more inventive writer than Shakespeare.

RANDALL WALLACE

The story of Wallace poured a Scottish prejudice in my veins which will boil along until the floodgates of life shut in eternal rest.

ROBERT BURNS

Hamilton's couplets are not the best poetry you will ever read, but they rattle along at a fair pace. In re-issuing this work, the publishers have re-opened the spring from which most of our conceptions of the Wallace legend come.

SCOTLAND ON SUNDAY

The return of Blind Harry's Wallace, a man who makes Mel look like a wimp.

THE SCOTSMAN

SOCIAL HISTORY

A Word for Scotland

Jack Campbell

with a foreword by Magnus Magnusson

ISBN 0 946487 48 0 PBK £12.99

'A word for Scotland' was Lord Beaverbrook's hope when he founded the *Scottish Daily Express*. That word for Scotland quickly became, and was for many years, the national newspaper of Scotland.

The pages of *A Word For Scotland* exude warmth and a wry sense of humour. Jack Campbell takes us behind the scenes to meet the larger-than-life characters and ordinary people who made and recorded the stories. Here we hear the stories behind the stories that hit the headlines in this great yarn of journalism in action.

It would be true to say 'all life is here'. From the Cheapside Street fire of which cost the lives of 19 Glasgow firemen, to the theft of the Stone of Destiny, to the lurid exploits of serial killer Peter Manuel, to encounters with world boxing champions Benny Lynch and Cassius Clay – this book offers telling glimpses of the characters, events, joy and tragedy which make up Scotland's story in the 20th century.

As a rookie reporter you were proud to work on it and proud to be part of it – it was fine newspaper right at the heartbeat of Scotland.

RONALD NEIL, Chief Executive of BBC Production, and a reporter on the *Scottish Daily Express* (1963-68)

This book is a fascinating reminder of Scottish journalism in its heyday. It will be read avidly by those journalists who take pride in their profession – and should be compulsory reading for those who don't.

JACK WEBSTER, columnist on *The Herald* and *Scottish Daily Express* journalist (1960-80)

The Crofting Years

Francis Thompson
ISBN 0 946487 06 5 PBK £6.95

Crofting is much more than a way of life. It is a storehouse of cultural, linguistic and moral values which holds together a scattered and struggling rural population. This book fills a blank in the written history of crofting over the last two centuries. Bloody conflicts and gunboat diploma-

cy, treachery, compassion, music and story: all figure in this mine of information on crofting in the Highlands and Islands of Scotland.

I would recommend this book to all who are interested in the past, but even more so to those who are interested in the future survival of our way of life and culture.
STORNOWAY GAZETTE

The book is a mine of information on many aspects of the past, among them the homes, the food, the music and the medicine of our crofting forebears.
John M Macmillan, erstwhile
CROFTERS COMMISSIONER FOR LEWIS AND HARRIS

Shale Voices

Alistair Findlay
foreword by Tam Dalyell MP
ISBN 0 946487 63 4 PBK £10.99
ISBN 0 946487 78 2 HBK £17.99

He was at Addiewell oil works. Anyone goes in there is there for keeps.

JOE, Electrician

There's shale from here to Ayr, you see.

DICK, a Drawer

The way I describe it is, you're a coal miner and I'm a shale miner. You're a tramp and I'm a toff.
HARRY, a Drawer

There were sixteen or eighteen Simpsons...
...She was having one every dividend we would say.
SISTERS, from Broxburn

Shale Voices offers a fascinating insight into shale mining, an industry that employed generations of Scots, had an impact on the social, political and cultural history of Scotland and gave birth to today's large oil companies. Author Alistair Findlay was born in the shale mining village of Winchburgh and is the fourth son of a shale miner, Bob Findlay, who became editor of the *West Lothian Courier*. *Shale Voices* combines oral history, local journalism and family history. The generations of communities involved in shale mining provide, in their own words, a unique documentation of the industry and its cultural and political impact.

Photographs, drawings, poetry and short stories make this a thought provoking and entertaining account. It is as much a joy to dip into and feast the eyes on as to read from cover to cover.

Alistair Findlay has added a basic source material to the study of Scottish History that is invaluable and will be of great benefit to future generations. Scotland owes him a debt of gratitude for undertaking this work.

TAM DALYELL MP

POETRY

Poems to be read aloud

Collected and with an introduction by Tom Atkinson
ISBN 0 946487 00 6 PBK £5.00

This personal collection of doggerel and verse ranging from the tear-jerking *Green Eye of the Yellow God* to the rarely printed, bawdy *Eskimo Nell* has a lively cult following. Much borrowed and rarely returned, this is a book for reading aloud in very good company, prefer-

ably after a dram or twa. You are guaranteed a warm welcome if you arrive at a gathering with this little volume in your pocket.

'This little book is an attempt to stem the great rushing tide of canned entertainment. A hopeless attempt of course. There is poetry of very high order here, but there is also some fearful doggerel. But that is the way of things. No literary axe is being ground.

Of course some of the items in this book are poetic drivel, if read as poems. But that is not the point. They all spring to life when they are read aloud. It is the combination of the poem with your voice, with all the art and craft you can muster, that produces the finished product and effect you seek.

You don't have to learn the poems. Why clutter up your mind with rubbish? Of course, it is a poorly furnished mind that doesn't carry a fair stock of poetry, but surely the poems to be remembered and savoured in secret, when in love, or ill, or sad, are not the ones you want to share with an audience.

So go ahead, clear your throat and transfix all talkers with a stern eye, then let rip!'
TOM ATKINSON

Luath Press Limited
committed to publishing well written books worth reading

LUATH PRESS takes its name from Robert Burns, whose little collie Luath (*Gael.*, swift or nimble) tripped up Jean Armour at a wedding and gave him the chance to speak to the woman who was to be his wife and the abiding love of his life. Burns called one of *The Twa Dogs* Luath after Cuchullin's hunting dog in *Ossian's Fingal*. Luath Press was established in 1981 in the heart of Burns country, and is now based a few steps up the road from Burns' first lodgings on Edinburgh's Royal Mile.
Luath offers you distinctive writing with a hint of unexpected pleasures.

Most bookshops in the UK, the US, Canada, Australia, New Zealand and parts of Europe either carry our books in stock or can order them for you. To order direct from us, please send a £sterling cheque, postal order, international money order or your credit card details (number, address of cardholder and expiry date) to us at the address below. Please add post and packing as follows: UK – £1.00 per delivery address; overseas surface mail – £2.50 per delivery address; overseas airmail – £3.50 for the first book to each delivery address, plus £1.00 for each additional book by airmail to the same address. If your order is a gift, we will happily enclose your card or message at no extra charge.

Luath Press Limited
543/2 Castlehill
The Royal Mile
Edinburgh EH1 2ND
Scotland
Telephone: 0131 225 4326 (24 hours)
Fax: 0131 225 4324
email: sales@luath.co.uk
Website: www.luath.co.uk